# Papa and Eva and Me

*By*

*Kate Lydon Varley*

# Dedication

In loving memory of Armando Raphael Carli and Eva Flax Carli

# Acknowledgments

Thanks to my writing friends for their help and encouragement, and for loving Papa and Eva.

Thanks to my children, John Varley and Maureen Ayers, who knew Eva and, to her delight, they called her Gigi.

And thanks to my husband Tom Varley, who has encouraged and supported me over the years, and continues to do so, no matter what idea I may come up with next.

# About the Author

Transplanted from Boston, Kate Lydon Varley has spend most of her adult life in Southeast Pennsylvania. She has worked in assembly at a toy factory; as a secretary; a story teller; a psychologist; a teacher. She was the founder and editor of the late, lamented Zine of Autobiographical Writing, Creek Road Gang; and she currently teaches autobiographical writing.

# 1

## First

When I was due to be born, my parents lived outside of Boston, but Papa, my maternal grandfather, was living and working in northern New Jersey. Of course, he didn't want to miss out on the birth of his first grandchild, so he came north in early August for the weekend I was due to be born.

The weekend came and went, and so did Papa, but I wasn't born.

So, he returned the following weekend, with, alas, a similar lack of results. But Papa was persistent, so he returned the third weekend in August, certain he'd go home a proud grandfather. Unfortunately, no such luck. Before returning to New Jersey that Sunday, an exasperated Papa asked my mother, "Isn't this baby ever going to be born?"

Tired of fruitless trips, he didn't travel north on the fourth weekend, so, of course, I was born that Saturday.

At the time, Papa and my maternal grandmother were living separately. They divorced when I was quite young, and shortly thereafter, Papa married Eva, who became part of the fabric of my family.

Papa, I've been told, was a doting grandfather, and remained so after the births of each of my four little brothers.

In those years, Papa changed jobs several times, each time requiring a long distance move. During most of my childhood, we'd see Papa once a year, generally in the summer.

In later years, no matter where they were living, Papa and Eva made annual visits to us, usually in August, often after their summer vacation on Lake George in New York.

We usually didn't know exactly when they'd arrive at our house, although my mother would prepare for weeks in advance, cleaning, cooking and stocking the freezer. Then we'd get a telephone call: they were on their way! Despite our excitement, we children would be bundled off to bed at our usual time, only to be awakened in the wee hours of the morning when Papa and Eva finally arrived. Sleepy-eyed and wearing our best pajamas, my little brothers and I would usually endure without complaint the sloppy wet kisses Papa and Eva gave. But should we wipe our faces after the kisses, we were sure to hear from Papa about it!

"What?" he would say, his voice deep and loud. "You're wiping off my kiss?" And of course, he'd kiss us again with another wet sloppy kiss.

And after Eva's kiss, she would rub her thumb at the skin around our mouths, trying to remove the traces of the deep red lipstick she always wore. It didn't come off our faces easily.

But after the yucky kissing ritual, they would give each of us kids a clear plastic case of chocolate cigarettes. We loved those chocolate cigarettes, and we were allowed to eat one of them right then, after which we were packed off to bed again, leaving the grown-ups to drink coffee and talk in the kitchen.

In the morning when we woke up, we'd find my mother in the kitchen making breakfast, and Papa at the kitchen table, smoking cigarettes, drinking coffee, talking, talking, talking.

# 2

# Papa the English Professor

Although both her parents had grown up in Malden, Massachusetts, my mother and her family lived in Buffalo, New York when she was a little girl. That was because Papa was then a professor of English at Canisius College.

"He couldn't get a job in Boston in those days," Mum told us, "because he was Italian. He had to go all the way to Buffalo to get a teaching job." She would then proudly tell us kids that Papa had not one degree, not two, not even three. No, Papa had four degrees: one bachelor's from the University of New Hampshire, two masters – one from the University of Arkansas, and one from Harvard! – and one doctorate, from the State University in Buffalo, New York.

Mum was tremendously proud of her brilliant father, and loved to brag about him. As a child, she had often met Papa's students, and they always made a big deal of their professor's little girl.

But having a grandfather who'd been an English professor was not always wonderful for me. When I was a child, should I ever make the teeniest grammatical slip, it was sure to become a federal case. "I cannot *believe* it!" my mother would say. "I cannot believe that *you, the granddaughter of an English professor*, would say that!" It wasn't all bad, though, I guess. Public humiliation of that kind melded me into a stickler for proper grammar.

There was a story related to Papa's years at Canisius that Mum loved to tell. Shortly before she and Dad got married, Mum had needed some dental work. Her mouth was too small for her teeth, she told us, and she was having a lot of pain. Although she was very afraid of dentists, she decided she had to do something about it, and maybe she'd even need to have some teeth pulled out! She chose a dentist in Malden, close to Mrs. Bell's Doughnut Shop, where my father made doughnuts and my mother waitressed. Dr. Rooney was a pleasant man who tried to put her at ease by making small talk. "Evelynn Carli," he said. "You know, when I was in college, I took an English course with a Professor Carli."

"My father was an English professor," Mum said.

"Oh, it wouldn't be the same man. I didn't go to school around here," Dr. Rooney said.

"Where did you go to school?" Mum asked.

“I went to Canisius College in Buffalo.”

“That’s where he taught! We lived in Buffalo when I was a little girl,” Mum said proudly. “You took that English course with my father!”

“You’re Professor Carli’s daughter?” Dr. Rooney asked.

“Yes! What a coincidence that you knew my father,” Mum said, and she began to relax. If Dr. Rooney had known Papa, surely he’d take good care of her. “Imagine that! Papa left Canisius years ago, and yet you still remember him.”

“Remember him?” Dr. Rooney said. “I’ll never forget him! He was one tough teacher, all right. You had to work hard for Professor Carli, and he never gave you a break.”

My mother nodded. Papa was loving, but strict.

“Yep,” Dr. Rooney said. “In all my years of school, he was the only one who ever gave me a grade of F!”

Mum’s anxiety level went way up again, but Dr. Rooney took good care of her dental problems nonetheless.

He became our family dentist, and never took it out on any of us that Papa had once flunked him years ago.

# 3

# Meal Planning with Papa

Although we usually saw Papa only once a year, I heard many stories about him year round from my mother. Not only was Papa brilliant, but it also seemed he knew how to do almost anything, and he was never shy about speaking up as needed.

*When I was a little girl in Buffalo,* my mother told me, *Papa planned our meals. Mama had no interest in what to buy or how to prepare it. It was Papa who did the food shopping, and he would bring my brother and me with him to the market every Saturday. He would take us to the deli counter, and he'd say to the man behind the counter, "What is that cheese there? Yes, that one. I'd like to sample it." The man would cut him a piece, and Papa would say, "The children will sample it too." The man would cut two more pieces, and we'd all taste it. Then Papa would say, "I'm not sure. What do you think, children? Shall we try a different one? What about this other cheese over here?" We might sample three or four cheeses before Papa decided which one to buy. And then he'd start on the deli meats and do the same thing. That man who worked at the meat and cheese counter must have hated to see us coming!*

*Mama didn't like to cook at all. She had never learned how to cook and she didn't care to. Papa would leave instructions for her when he went to work, telling her what to make for our dinner that night, and how to prepare it with groceries he'd bought on the weekend. But Mama's attempts often didn't turn out very well.*

*I think the worst time, though, was when one of Papa's students had gone hunting, and he made Papa a gift of a goose he had shot. Mama was so upset about having to prepare it! She had to take the feathers off it and everything! Papa thought it was only right to invite the young man to dinner to enjoy the goose with the family. There we were, Papa, my brother and me sitting in the dining room with the young man. When Mama put that goose on the table, it was full of buckshot. Every piece of meat had buckshot! I didn't want to eat it, and Mama didn't want to either! But we had to, because we couldn't offend the guest. But it was awful!*

*My brother and I always had to eat everything we were given, like it or not. Any time I didn't clean my plate at dinner, I got the same food on the same plate again the next morning for breakfast, and, if I still didn't eat all of it, again for lunch, and for every meal, until I finally did finish it. Fish, goose with buckshot, anything! There was nothing else on the menu until I ate everything that my parents had put on my plate for me to eat.*

# 4

# The Trip to Chicago

When I was three, almost four, my parents, my baby brother Johnny and I traveled by train from Boston to Chicago to visit Papa and Eva.

My mother had brought a big lunch for us – sandwiches, hard-boiled eggs, fruit and cookies to eat on the train. But not milk, although I always drank milk, and of course, Baby Johnny needed milk for his bottles. We hadn't brought any milk with us, though, because we could get it, fresh and cold, on the train. The only problem was that, in order to get it, my mother had to go to the dining car. Daddy would stay with Johnny and keep our seats for us, but Mummy would take me with her every time she went to get milk. Mummy would hold my hand and we'd walk through our car on the train to the door at the front end. When Mummy opened that door, there would be a big rush of air, and then we had to step from one car to the next on the noisy, bumpy train. When we were in between the cars, I'd get scared every time that we might fall off the train, or even fall under the train! I didn't want to go on those trips to the dining car, but Baby Johnny needed his bottle, so there we'd be, Mummy and me, almost getting killed just to get milk for baby Johnny.

But when we could just stay in our seats, the train was fun. Mummy and Daddy would tell me stories or read books to me, and we could look out the windows at all kinds of things, or we could watch the other people on the train. There was a big family in our car, with lots and lots of kids who were always getting up and moving around, making noise, tripping over things, and getting into trouble. Their Mummy didn't have any lunch for them, and she didn't go to the dining car to get milk or to get them anything to eat. When we opened up our lunch, one of their kids came over and stood watching us eat. Daddy used to be poor when he was a little boy, and he felt bad for that family, so he gave him some of our sandwiches and some cookies.

When night came, it was dark in the train car, and we slept in our seats. In the middle of the night, we all woke up when someone started yelling. It turned out that one of the kids from that big family who didn't have lunches fell asleep lying on the floor of the train, and the conductor didn't see him and stepped on him by accident.

But finally we got to Chicago, and Papa was there to pick us up from the train. I don't remember everything that happened, but there were four great things about Chicago, but there were also two things that weren't so good.

Every morning we were there, Eva made us bacon and eggs for breakfast. At home, I had toast or cereal in the morning, so bacon and eggs, especially bacon, was a great breakfast! And at home every morning, I had to drink grapefruit juice, which I hated, but every day we were in Chicago, Eva gave me orange juice, and I loved it. She might get lipstick all over you, but the breakfasts she made were so good!

The second great thing was that Papa took us to the big zoo in Chicago. I loved going to the zoo, and I got even more excited when Papa told me this zoo had a laughing hyena. I had never seen a laughing hyena, and I could hardly wait, because I never ever had heard any animal laugh. And that was the first not so good thing in Chicago. The laughing hyena just walked back and forth and back in forth in his cage, and he never laughed, not even once, so I didn't get to hear the hyena laugh.

I found out the third great thing about Chicago when I went out with Papa in his backyard that night. There were lots of tiny lights flashing on and off in his yard, and Papa told me that they were fireflies. I had never seen a firefly before, and it was like magic. Papa said that the lights the fireflies had were a way insects made friends. I was so lucky to be able to watch those little fireflies making friends by blinking their little lights in Papa's back yard! We never had that at home!

It was almost my fourth birthday when we went to Chicago, and Papa and Eva gave me my birthday present early, the night before we were leaving to go home. They gave me a real majorette costume! It had a big tall hat, just like majorettes wore in parades, and a beautiful real uniform, creamy-colored shiny cloth with big buttons on the front. That was the fourth and best surprise about Chicago. I got to wear it that night, as soon as I opened the box. It was the most exciting present I'd ever got!

But the second bad thing happened the next day, when it was time to go home. I wanted to wear my majorette costume on the train, so everyone could see me in it. Papa would have let me, and Eva would have too, but Mummy said no, and that was that. She packed it up and put it in a suitcase. I had to go home looking like I was just a regular little girl, but instead, even though I couldn't wear my costume on the train so no one on the train got to see it, I was a real majorette anyway.

# 5

# Fine Dining

During his visits when I was little, Papa would always say, "You know, I'd like to take everyone out to dinner tonight, but I just don't know anywhere we could go. Does anyone know a good restaurant?"

I'd look from one grown-up to another.

"I don't know," Mummy would say.

"I can't think of one," Daddy would say.

How could they forget, I'd wonder.

"If only we knew of a good restaurant," Papa would say sadly.

"I know where we can go!" I would cry.

"You know a good restaurant, Kay?" Papa would ask. "Tell me, what is it?"

"Howard Johnson's!" I'd announce.

"And they have good food, do they?" he'd ask.

"Yes, Papa," I'd say.

"If we go to this place – what was its name?"

"Howard Johnson's!" I'd repeat.

"Howard Johnson's." Papa would nod. "Well, if we go to this Howard Johnson's, Kay, what would you order for dinner?"

"A Howard Johnson's hot dog!" I'd shout.

Who knows why, but the grown-ups would all laugh, and before long, we'd all climb into Papa's big car and head out to my favorite restaurant in the whole world where I would get the best hot dog ever.

# 6

# Eva and the Toothbrush

Usually at home, I had toast and Rice Krispies and stupid grapefruit juice for breakfast, but when Papa and Eva visited us, breakfast would be a feast, with orange juice, bacon and eggs and toast, sometimes pancakes or waffles too. And my father would bring a few dozen doughnuts from work. Eva took bacon and eggs in stride, because she made them every day at home, but she was always delighted with the doughnuts. Although she usually had little interest in talking with Dad, she'd quiz him about doughnuts. – *What kind is that one? Which ones are filled? Do any have cream filling? What kind of cream? What kind of frosting is that? Are there any jellies? Any unusual jellies?* And then, in the first sacrilege of many to come, she would begin to cut pieces from various doughnuts, trying a bit of this and a bit of that, until there were perhaps a half dozen doughnuts with pieces missing, all beginning to get stale, and, as far as we kids were concerned, getting spoiled for the rest of us.

One year, as Papa sat at the table after breakfast, smoking and drinking coffee and talking, Eva excused herself to go "get ready." We kids knew what that meant. We had only one bathroom, and Eva was going to be in it for at least an hour. And Papa would still be talking when she finally came back. Meanwhile, my brothers and I were going to sit at the table, listening to Papa, and keeping an eye on the doughnut box in case having good manners might get us more doughnuts.

But this day, suddenly we heard Eva's slippers pelting back towards the kitchen, even though she never got ready that fast at our house. But there she was, toothbrush in one hand, tube in the other, and foam oozing from her mouth, and she was crying, "Oh, Pat!"

"What is it, darling?" Papa sounded worried. We all were!

"I was brushing my teeth, Pat," Eva wailed. "I took a tube from the medicine chest and squeezed it out onto my brush and I started brushing. But I didn't realize that the tube didn't have toothpaste in it, Pat. It's hair cream! And it's burning my mouth!"

"You damn fool!" Papa barked. "Go rinse your mouth out!" And having issued orders, he went back to talking with my mother.

"Oh, Pat!" Crying even harder, Eva returned to the bathroom.

We kids had to work hard at saying nothing and keeping a straight face, but we did it, because we knew that if any of us had shown even the tiniest grin, forget about more doughnuts! We would have been in big trouble with Mum!

# 7

# Papa the Pagan

During one of his visits, early on a summer Sunday morning, Papa drove us to Mass. We all piled into his car, my mother explaining that she'd get breakfast ready as soon as we returned, and that there was freshly made coffee in the meantime. Papa dropped us off at the church, the car motor still running as we got out. I was the last one out of the car.

"Won't you come to Mass with us, Papa?" I asked.

"No, Kay," Papa answered. "I'm not a Catholic. I'm a pagan. But you say a little prayer to your god for me."

"I will, Papa," I said.

"I'm going to run an errand while you're in church. I have to pick up my racing paper, but I'll be waiting for you when you get out of church. Look for my car."

"I will, Papa," I said

As he drove off, I hurried into the church, but my head was spinning.

Papa was a pagan?

I had learned about pagans in my class in Catholic school. Pagans had false gods! They worshipped golden idols and danced around fires! And they were on the wrong side of all kinds of things in the Old Testament. I thought they died out a long time ago. To think that they still existed! And – what was even more astounding – to hear from his very own lips that my grandfather was one of them! It was the kind of news that I wanted to tell someone, and I was very much tempted to tell some of my friends from school, but I decided not to, because what would they think of me if I told them my grandfather was a Pagan!

When I later told my mother about it, she explained to me that Papa wasn't really a pagan; he just didn't believe in God. I was relieved. It didn't bother me that Papa wasn't a believer. I figured that someday Papa would change his mind, and then God would take him back, just like a father forgave the Prodigal son, who wasted all the money his father gave him, and then came home to be forgiven and get a party and lots of other good stuff from his father. And when the son who had been good all along complained, he was the one who got in trouble. That story of the prodigal son never sounded to me like a very fair story though, because the naughty kid got a special party and the good kid just got yelled at. It sounded like something that would happen to me. But if that story would save Papa, something good would have come out of it, so maybe Papa would be a Prodigal son someday.

I didn't start to worry too much about Papa until I learned about the way the Catholic Church thought about people getting a divorce.

It seemed to me that one of the worst things in the world that could happen to a kid was to have parents who got divorced. Mum told me lots of times about how hard it was for her that her parents argued and got divorced, and how lucky I was that my parents loved each other and stayed together.

So it seemed like divorce was a pretty bad thing, but what seemed to get God really mad at you was if you married someone else after you got divorced, unless your husband or wife died, and then it was okay to get married again. Grandma was divorced from Papa, but she didn't get married again, so it seemed like God didn't care so much about her side of the divorce. He let her go to church all the time, and he'd let her into heaven too, someday when she died. But things were a lot different for Papa. As soon as he married Eva, Papa wasn't even allowed to go into a church. He was excommunicated, which meant that they threw him out! I didn't think that Papa could even go inside the church building anymore, and if he tried to, someone would probably chase him away. And besides that, God didn't let divorced people into heaven if they got married to someone else after they got divorced!

How could I ever be happy in heaven, I wondered, if my very own grandfather was suffering in hell for ever and ever? Did God think I could just forget about Papa, that I would never miss him? It seemed to me that God might be getting carried away sometimes on punishments for people, and maybe going to heaven really wasn't all it was cracked up to be.

# 8

# Uncle Guido and Aunt Aurelia

When Papa and Eva visited us, we usually set aside a day for going with them to see Uncle Guido and Aunt Aurelia.

Papa was born in Massachusetts, but his mother and father were born in San Severo, Italy. His father, Vincenzo, came to America before anyone else in the family came. He found a place to live, and he started a business making hats in Boston, while Papa's mother, Graziella, waited behind in Italy with her two sons – Alfredo and Guido. It took a few years before he had enough money, but finally Vincenzo sent for Graziella to come to America. Alfredo, the oldest boy, stayed in Italy, and the family wanted him to become a soldier because that was a good way to get an education, so Alfredo never came to America. Guido, the younger boy, who was only five years old then, was left behind, and he went to live with Graziella's brother, Uncle the Priest, who wanted to prepare Guido to become a priest too. So when Graziella finally got to come to American, she left Alfredo and Guido behind, but she brought the two other children, Gino, who in America was called Gene,  and Ottavio, who was always called Tav. And there were two children born in America: Papa, and his younger sister Algesa.

It turned out that Uncle Guido didn't become a priest, though. Uncle the Priest tried to help him to learn to be a priest, but it didn't work. When Guido was a young man, Uncle the Priest wrote to his sister Graziella and told her that Guido liked the girls, so he wouldn't make it as a priest. So Guido was sent to America to live with his family.

Vincenzo Carli, Guido's and Papa's father, was a hatter by trade. When Papa was a little boy, Vincenzo had his own shop on Beacon Hill in Boston. He had bought a hat business from its owner, lock, stock, barrel, and name too, which is how Vincenzo Carli, and later, his son Guido with him, became the owners of Kelly's Hats. Mum told me that in those days, it was better to have an Irish name than an Italian one, because lots of people in Boston were prejudiced against Italians.

Guido joined his father in the business, and became an expert hatter.

Sometimes, when I was little, Mum would take us kids along when she went shopping in Boston. We would always stop at Kelly's Hats on Beacon Hill. The shop was partway below the level of the sidewalk, so from outside we could look down through the windows to see the cases, the racks of hats, and Uncle Guido.

Visiting Uncle Guido at work was very exciting. The shop always seemed dark to me, but it was fun to go there, because we could look up at feet and legs hurrying along outside. The shop had all kinds of odd smells from the making of hats. Uncle Guido, wearing a gray work apron, would come from behind the counter, hug and kiss my mother, and then he would pinch our cheeks, my brothers and me, talking all the time!

Papa once told me that after Guido came to this country, his father decided to arrange a marriage for him. Vincenzo knew of a young woman who was a nice girl, and it was decided that her family would bring her to a certain place in Boston at a certain time on a certain day. Uncle Guido was to walk by, look at the young woman, and report back to his father whether he thought she would be acceptable as a bride. Guido walked by, and he thought the young woman looked quite nice. He said he would marry her before he even got to say hello to her. So it was arranged for Aurelia Provo to marry Guido Carli.

I had known Uncle Guido and Aunt Aurelia all my life.

Uncle Guido had a very loud voice, and he loved to pinch children's cheeks. I remember him saying that my brothers and I were his favorite children, because we didn't shrink away or cry when he pinched our cheeks like other children did. He pinched very hard, but he was my mother's favorite uncle, and Mum warned us that we were to put up with it when Uncle Guido' pinched our cheeks, and no crying either, or else we'd be in big trouble with her!

Aunt Aurelia was quiet and sweet, and almost always busy doing something, but she was never too busy to tell Uncle Guido to stop pinching the children's cheeks. "You frighten them," she'd say.

"Not these children," he'd tell her. "Evelyn's children aren't afraid of me. They like me."

"They love you," my mother would say, and we would smile and nod, hoping there would be no more pinches. Then my brothers would go off to chase each other in the yard, or maybe to play with Lad. Lad was Uncle Guido's German shepherd. My mother had told us that Uncle Guido always had a German shepherd named Lad. When one Lad got old and died, Uncle Guido would get a new German shepherd, and name the new dog Lad. There was a story in the family about one Lad from when my mother was a little girl. It seemed that one day, Aunt Aurelia and Uncle Guido had gone out, leaving Lad in the fenced-in yard. When they returned, they found the yard dotted with dollar bills and change, along with a tambourine. They guessed that someone, perhaps from the Salvation Army, had been going from house to house asking for donations that he would put in a tambourine he carried. Lad probably saw him and chased him away, and he dropped all his money and his tambourine when he ran away.

The Lad we knew might have been a good guard dog too, but he was gentle with my brothers. I kept my distance from him, though, because I was afraid of German shepherds. Luckily, Aunt

Aurelia would invite me to come with her into the kitchen. She and I would talk together while she cooked and baked and got dinner ready, and sometimes I helped her. It was always easy and comfortable talking with her.

When I was almost five, my brother Kevin was born, and our mother asked Aunt Aurelia to be Kevin's godmother. Aunt Aurelia happily agreed. On the day of his Christening, he was only a few weeks old. Aunt Aurelia was holding baby Kevin when he suddenly spit up on her. Mum got very embarrassed! But Aunt Aurelia didn't seem to mind at all. She wiped baby Kevin and herself, and patted Kevin's back, cuddling him, and talking to him and singing to him.

Every summer, when we visited Uncle Guido, we would go to Burlington, Massachusetts, to the house Uncle Guido and Aunt Aurelia had built themselves. Uncle Guido had done the carpentry, but my mother told me that Aunt Aurelia had put in all the plumbing by herself! This was quite surprising, especially since Aunt Aurelia seemed nothing like a plumber. She was a little lady and she always seemed quiet and sweet. She sewed and she cooked. She didn't use patterns to make clothing like my mother did. Aunt Aurelia could just measure a person and figure out how to make something that fit them and looked beautiful. And she was a very good cook. She made her own pasta, and I also remember her making pizza, which was not round, but like a rectangle. She, Uncle Guido and Papa all pronounced the word pizza a little differently from everyone else I knew. They would say – pee – et – za. One time, I heard someone say that Italians don't really eat pizza, but I knew that wasn't true, because I watched Aunt Aurelia make pizza, and then we all ate it.

When we visited Uncle Guido and Aunt Aurelia in the summer, they would set up a large table outside for the meal Aunt Aurelia would serve us. Sometimes their grown sons would join us; they didn't have any daughters. There was always lots of talking going on while we ate. When he stayed at our house, Papa always had the loudest voice, but at Uncle Guido's house, Papa was quieter. He didn't talk as much as usual, but he asked more questions. Eva was quiet too, and so were my parents. Uncle Guido was Papa's big brother, already a man when Papa had been just a boy, and everyone respected him and loved him.

When Vincenzo, Papa's and Guido's father, decided to move back to Italy, he wanted to bring his two youngest children, Papa and Algesa, who was Papa's younger sister. Papa was a teenager then, and he refused to go. "You're an Italian," he told his father, "but I was born here and I'm an American. Italy may be your country, but this is my country, and I'm staying here." Vincenzo couldn't get Papa to change his mind, and in the end, he took Algesa with him back to Italy, and left Papa in the care of Guido and Aurelia. Papa lived with them until he went away to college.

Grownups always called Papa "Pat," except for Uncle Guido and Aunt Aurelia. They called him Armando, which was his Italian name. Whenever we went to Uncle Guido's house with Papa, Uncle Guido was happy to see him, and proud of him proud of him, and he always told him stories about their family in Italy.

He told stories of Uncle the Priest and other family in Italy that we never met. I remember Uncle Guido showing Papa a large document. "Look at this, Armando!" he said. "Uncle the Priest sent me a family tree!" It was made up mostly of people I had never heard of. Uncle Guido excitedly explained who was who, and where each person fit in, while Papa nodded, looked over the family tree, and sometimes he asked a question. They studied that paper until dinner was ready, and they went back to it later, in the twilight.

I would often leave the grownups listening to Uncle Guido, and instead I would go with Aunt Aurelia to the kitchen. She would talk with me, making me feel almost like I was a grownup too.

But when we all sat down together to eat, the grownups would drink wine with dinner, wine that Uncle Guido made himself, from grapes he grew in his own grape arbor. And every year, he would give my mother a bottle of his wine. Mum drank wine one time a year, on New Year's Eve, when she'd celebrate with some of Uncle Guido's wine that she poured into a glass filled mostly with ginger ale.

Uncle Guido and Aunt Aurelia grew a lot of vegetables as well as fruit in the warm weather, and they had done that for years. Mum told me that when she was a little girl, she would stay with them overnight sometimes. One morning after breakfast, she decided to pick a bouquet of flowers for Aunt Aurelia from their gardens. When Mum gave Aunt Arelia the big bouquet she picked, Aunt Aurelia thanked her, but she told her next year, choose flowers from a different part of the yard, because these were strawberry flowers, and that meant there would be no strawberries to eat this year. But Aunt Arelia made sure to tell Mum that she understood, and it was all right.

The summer days when we would visit Uncle Guido and Aunt Aurelia at their house, we would get there in the afternoon and stay until well past sunset, but finally it would be time to go home. Uncle Guido and Aunt Aurelia would kiss us, and Uncle Guido might give us another pinch or two. Papa and his big brother would hug. Then, we would wave goodbye, blow kisses, and go home.

# 9

# Gifts from Papa and Eva

Every Christmas Papa and Eva sent money for us kids. During my very early childhood, they mailed a lump sum check for my parents to use to get something for us that we'd like. In later years, the family would receive a fat envelope with individual checks for each child. The first check I remember getting was for five dollars, with checks in the same amount for each of my brothers. When we talked to Papa and Eva on the phone that Christmas morning, wishing them a Merry Christmas, and thanking them for the check, we were already thinking about how we'd spend our riches. What wonders we could find at the Five and Ten, well under the grand sum of five dollars! We were usually able to get a few things each, and maybe have a little left over for a candy bar. By the time I was in high school, our checks were for seven-fifty each, enabling me to buy myself several paperback books, or perhaps some art supplies, while my brothers often concentrated on sporting goods.

But for my birthday in the years before I got to be a teenager, I didn't get a check. Papa and Eva usually would send a package in the mail. One August, I think the year I turned six, I opened my birthday package and discovered inside a sewing machine that looked like a miniature version of my mother's. Although it was child-sized, I saw on it all the features that would make it really work -- a place to put the spool of thread, a shining silvery needle, a wheel on the side of the machine that could make the needle go up and down, an electric cord. I was thrilled, imagining all the wonderful clothes I could make for my dolls. When I asked my mother to help me use it, she told me that the instructions for it were in German, and so, there was nothing to be done; it was a useless gift. From time to time, I looked at it, way up on a shelf in my closet, but eventually it disappeared without me ever getting a chance to use it.

For my seventh birthday, the box Papa and Eva sent was a different shape, with the disappointing oblong appearance that usually meant clothing. Inside was a long-sleeved wool sweater. I was pleased to see that, unlike all my other sweaters, this was a pullover, not a cardigan. I liked its bright color, so different from the blue or white cardigans my mother always got for me to wear with my blue and white school uniform.

"Screaming orange," my mother said. "That's Eva for you. Their couch is orange, their curtains are orange, she'd paint everything orange if she could. Orange is such an inferior color, but it figures it would be *her* favorite."

Until that very moment, I hadn't known that orange was an inferior color. And now I had an inferior-colored orange sweater!

At my school, we were allowed to wear our costumes the day of our class Halloween party. Usually my mother would make up costumes for us at home, and change our faces with make-up. But that October, our household was busy with my third brother, who was only four months old, and Mum decided to buy me a mask. For my school party, and also for trick-or-treating that night, I wore a gray skirt, my birthday inferior-colored orange wool sweater, and a jack-o-lantern mask. After that, my mother packed the sweater away, and I never saw it again, which was too bad, because I liked that sweater even though it was orange.

Another year, Papa and Eva's gift was a sterling silver bracelet, engraved with a name. My given name was Kathleen, and that's what Grandma, Papa's first wife, always called me, as did the nuns who taught me at school, and it was what my mother called me when she was angry with me. My father, my brothers, and almost all our family and friends called me Kay, and my mother often did so too, although she was just as likely to call me Kitty, Kitten, Katie or Kate.

The pretty little letters engraved on the gift bracelet said "Kathy." It was puzzling to me. No one called me Kathy. Although I thanked Papa and Eva for the gift, I seldom wore it, because it seemed to me to have someone else's name on it.

A more successful gift was another bracelet Papa and Eva sent me, which was similar to a charm bracelet, but had coins of different countries in place of charms. I looked at all of them, and discovered that one of the coins was from Brazil, where Papa had spent a year during World War II. I was delighted to have the coin from Brazil, and all those other coins too. Somehow that bracelet seemed to link me to Papa and his time in Brazil for the USO. I was proud to wear that bracelet. It lost a few coins over the years, but I still have that bracelet with its Brazilian coin safely tucked away in my jewelry box.

# 10

## Getting to Know Eva

My mother always spoke in glowing terms about her brilliant, beloved father. Papa was charmingly eccentric, something that came with his great intelligence, she'd suggest, but she wasn't as complimentary about Eva. Mum thought Eva was sort of strange or difficult. Papa was knowledgeable, and had many strong and well-thought-out positions, but as Mum saw it, Eva just had opinions, and altogether too many of them.

Papa's divorce from my grandmother felt bitterly recent to my mother. I can't remember anyone having told me this, but it was quite clear in my mind, even as a young child, that Papa was my grandfather, but that Eva was really *not* my grandmother. I was to be polite and respectful to all adults, but the focus of their visits to us in Massachusetts, for my mother as well as for us kids, was that *Papa* was coming. Eva was part of the package, and although we welcomed her, it was not always with a feeling of open arms.

Nonetheless, whenever Papa and Eva came to visit my family, we pulled out the red carpet. My parents gave up their bed, sleeping in the living room so Papa and Eva would have their bedroom. Even breakfast became a feast when they visited, and we'd have extra things like potato salad at lunch. The dinners Mum made for them were things she planned weeks in advance, and often included things we never had just for us, like, for instance, zucchini. And, of course, whether or not it involved food, we'd take Papa and Eva on lots of outings too.

But my conversations with Eva often didn't go easily.

During one of those outings, I fell and cut my knee on gravel as we were walking from a parking lot uphill to the place where we planned to picnic. Eva, who was just in front of me, turned and saw the cut, which was bleeding a little.

"What happened to you?" she demanded.

"I fell down."

"You fell? But you didn't even cry!" she exclaimed. "How am I supposed to know that you got hurt if you don't even cry?"

"It's not that bad." I was about twelve at the time, and had long since given up wailing over every scrape.

"That is the most ridiculous thing! You should cry when you get hurt! The next time you fall down, you make sure you cry!"

Another time, Eva took me aside so that we could have a little talk and get to know each other better. She chattily asked, "Which one of your brothers do you have the most trouble getting along with?"

At the time, my brother John and I got along like cats and dogs, but I wouldn't have told that to an outsider for the world.

"None of them," I said. "I love all my brothers."

"Well, there must be at least one that you argue with!" she insisted.

"No," I lied. "We all get along."

As Eva was not a person to give up easily, she continued to quiz me about my brothers' presumed bad habits, while I stubbornly insisted that my brothers were without fault. Eva seemed quite bothered with me about it, but I wouldn't change my story.

Dad also had trouble talking with Eva. He was a soft-spoken man, On another of Papa and Eva's visits, my parents had planned a trip to Good Harbor Beach in Gloucester. Dad was driving, with Eva in the front seat beside him, because it would be more comfortable for her. As we set off, he asked, "Would you like me to go the fastest way – it's all highway – or, should we take the scenic route? It takes longer, but you get more ocean views."

"Oh, the scenic route!" Eva cried.

And then, as we wound our way north through the small towns lining the coast, Eva sat with her arms crossed over her chest, commenting loudly, "I don't see what's so scenic about this. This doesn't look nice at all! I thought we were going to see the ocean."

"The road will wind back to the ocean," Dad said.

"But most of the time, we can't see the ocean at all! I don't see why you call it scenic, Jack! It's not scenic at all!"

I could see my father was doing a slow burn, but he said nothing.

When we stopped at a gas station, we all waited in the hot car while Eva went in to use the restroom. She returned about fifteen minutes later. "That was the strangest restroom I've ever seen!" she declared. "When I went in, the lights came on and piped-in music started up. I was sitting there in the bathroom, minding my own business, and all of a sudden, the music stopped and it went totally black! Not a light in the place!"

"They must have had a timer for the lights, darling," Papa suggested.

"Did you ever hear of such a thing! A timer in a restroom! Is it always like this in New England?"

We stopped at a clam shack for lunch, a simple place with great seafood, my parents said, although I couldn't swear to that myself, since I always got a hot dog. It turned out that the place just wasn't up to Eva's standards, and she complained about it the rest of the way to Gloucester.

Once we reached the beach, Dad went into the water with us kids while my mother spent time with Papa and Eva. Dad was always polite to people, and he tried with Eva, but she was not polite to him.

I remember Eva in her dark sunglasses and bathing suit, her thin legs, feet pointing in opposite directions, and her straight-legged from the hip shuffle as she walked the beach, talking continually to my unusually quiet mother. Since Papa also talked continually, I don't know how my mother could follow either monologue, except for the moments when Papa and Eva got angry and started arguing with each other.

On the way home, we stopped for a great treat: ice cream at Dick and June's, where they had just about any flavor of ice cream you could think of. As my father was pulling into a parking spot, Eva, sitting in the front seat beside him, said, "I don't see why you're parking here, Jack! That spot over there is much closer to the place!"

My father had had enough. "For God's sake, park it yourself!" he said. He shut off the car, left the keys in the ignition, got out and walked away.

"What is the matter with Jack?" Eva asked. "Does he always do this?"

Another time, we took Papa and Eva to a different ice cream place, Putnam's Pantry, which had a wonderful ice cream smorgasbord. We could choose our size of sundae and order any flavor of ice cream, after which we could pick from about a zillion toppings – chocolate, fruits, nuts, candies, hot fudge, butterscotch and fruit toppings, syrups, marshmallow, whipped cream, sprinkles – anything we could think of, and some things we had never imagined. Having noticed Eva's sweet tooth, my mother thought the place would particularly please her; she'd be able to make her own sundae with as many toppings as she liked. We kids loved the rare occasion when we went to Putman's Pantry, so were thrilled, and Eva seemed intrigued, at least until she got into an argument with the young man behind the counter.

"I want a small ice cream," Eva said, "but I want it in a large dish."

"If you want a large dish, I have to give you a large ice cream," the young man told her.

"I don't want a large ice cream. I want a small ice cream. But I want a large dish."

"We can't do that," the young man said. "I can only give you a large dish if you get a large ice cream."

"That's very foolish," Eva told him. "I'm not interested in the ice cream. It's the toppings that I like! That's why I want the large dish! I want to have room for lots of toppings! So I want my serving of ice cream to be small!"

"If you want a small ice cream, I have to give you a small dish."

While the line grew behind us, Eva continued to argue her point, while the clerk kept saying that the rule was he could only give someone a large dish if they were asking for a large ice cream. He had to give large for large, and small for small. We kids were getting more and more worried that we'd never get our ice cream! Finally, to our great relief, Eva agreed to get a small ice cream in a small dish. But she complained throughout the toppings smorgasbord, and all through eating. "I can't try even half the toppings I want!" she exclaimed, as we watched the heaps of goo dripping from her dish onto the metal tray below. "They're very unreasonable here. Are they always like this? I don't know why you come here!"

# 11

# Shady Dealings

During Papa and Eva's annuals visits, we sometimes made a trip to one of our favorite beaches, Good Harbor beach in Gloucester. The water was always clear and cold, the beach sandy, rather than rocky, the waves big enough to make them fun for jumping, and the shells that washed up on the beach were varied. One year, as we trekked from the parking area to the sandy beach, Papa noticed a shop which rented out beach umbrellas for the day.

"Do you want to get an umbrella?" Papa asked my mother.

"I don't think so. We never get one, Papa," my mother said.

"Jackie and the children are very fair," Papa said. He always called my father Jackie. "You and I tan, of course, and Eva too, but I don't want Jackie or the children to get a burn."

"I brought long-sleeved shirts for them to put on," my mother said.

"Long-sleeved shirts! Hell!" Papa said. "I'm going to get an umbrella!"

I don't know what the cost of rental was, but my mother remarked that it was a lot to pay to use an umbrella for a few hours.

"I'll take care of it," Papa said as he took out his wallet, which was always fat with dollars. The next thing we knew, Papa had obtained for us a large green and white canvas umbrella. When we spread out our blankets to sit on, Papa made a hole in the sand and set up the umbrella at a jaunty angle. What a treat! It was so big that all of us kids could fit in the shady spot it made. And when we ran down to the water, or walked along the beach looking for shells, or went to the food stand, we could always see where our blanket was, because it was marked by that big green and white umbrella.

We had a wonderful day, and stayed long after most people had left the beach. Finally, we packed up our things, Papa picked up the umbrella, and we began the trek back to the parking lot, slogging along through dry, shifting dune sand.

But, surprise of all surprises, when we arrived at the shop that rented umbrellas so that we could return it, they were closed!

"Damnedest thing!" Papa said.

"What are we going to do about the umbrella?" my mother exclaimed.

"We'll take it with us, of course," Papa said. "That'll fit in the back of the wagon, won't it, Jackie?" Papa asked my father.

"I guess so," Dad said, his forehead all scrunched up.

I was shocked. It couldn't be that Papa was telling us to steal the umbrella!

Nonetheless, Papa carried the umbrella back to the car, and we all got in while he and Dad packed all of our bags and bundles, along with the green and white umbrella, into the back of our station wagon.

Thereafter, for years, my family had a big green and white umbrella that we brought with us to the beach. It was wonderful to have the shade, but I always felt sort of guilty about it.

It wasn't until much, much later that I began to wonder. Papa loved to play tricks on us. Would he really have stolen that umbrella, or had Papa bought it for us as a surprise?

I don't know for sure, because I never asked him, but I have my suspicions.

# 12

## Timely Changes

My mother was named after her mother, Evelyn. They were both named Evelyn Ruth, and as a child, my mother would use "Junior" after her name, as her brother signed his name as Armando Ralph Junior. When she was a child, her parents always called her "Baby Evelyn," or just "Baby." When I was a little girl, Mum's mother and brother, her aunts and her uncles and her cousins, had all moved on from that, and they called her "Evie."

But not Papa.

"What time does Jackie get home from work, Baby?"

"The children grew so much this year, Baby!"

That's what Papa always called my mother – "Baby."

One summer, when Papa and Eva came for their visit, Mum had a talk with her father about the matter.

"Papa," she said, "I'm thirty years old now."

"So you are, Baby," he agreed. "So you are."

"I'm grown up now, Papa. I don't think you should call me 'Baby' anymore."

"No?" Papa asked.

"No. I'm an adult, and I don't want to be called 'Baby!'"

"Hmmm," Papa said. "What shall I call you then?"

"I want you to call me 'Evie.'"

Papa nodded. "Reasonable," he said. "Fine. Evie. That's what I'll call you."

"Good," she said.

"Well, Evie, how about another cup of coffee?" Papa asked.

"I've got some on the stove, Papa," she said. "Give me your cup." But as she reached for it, my mother looked into his face and exclaimed, "Papa! What happened to your moustache?"

"About time! I was wondering when you'd notice," he said.

"You shaved your moustache off this morning?" she said. "I can't believe it! You've had a moustache all my life!"

"This morning!" Papa said. "Hell, no. I shaved it off over a year ago."

"A year ago, Papa? Didn't you have a moustache when you came last summer?"

"No, I shaved it off that spring, so this is my second summer without the moustache."

"And I didn't even notice last year that it was gone," Mum said.

"Eva wanted to tell you, but I told her not to," Papa said. "I wanted to see how long it took you to notice the difference."

# 13

## Our Street

The house where we lived for the first eleven years of my life was on Biltmore Street, a tiny, dead-end street off Pleasant. On Pleasant Street at our corner, there was a car dealer on one side, and a Jenny gas station on the other. Our house was just behind the Jenny station's white picket back fence, where lots of blue-flowering chicory bloomed every summer. There were three houses on our side, two of which were owned by our landlord, and the third of which belonged to two snooty old ladies who never said hello, but who sat on their front porch and complained loudly to each other that the other people living on the street had no manners. Opposite us on Biltmore, there was a long, one-story building which housed several businesses, then a parking lot, and, near the end of the street, a gun club, outside of which I could find lots of metal casings lying in the parking lot and on the street. It always seemed they must be good for something, so I used to collect them, although I never found much to do with them. Biltmore Street ended at the tall barbed-wire topped chain-link fence surrounding the Malden High School Football Stadium.

I remember standing outside our house, all of us saying our good-byes to Papa and Eva at the end of one of their summer visits. As usual, there were those messy, wet kisses that made me wish I could wipe my face, but I didn't want Papa to think I was wiping his kiss away, because I wouldn't do that, so I'd try to put up with it until he wasn't looking. Papa would assure us he would call us as soon as they got back home, to let us know they had arrived home, safe and sound. My mother would smile, her eyes shiny with tears. There would be encouragements to us kids to work hard in school, and to write letters to Papa and Eva, to tell them about what we were doing. And eventually, Papa would usher Eva into the car, they'd wave and blow kisses, and then they were gone.

We'd go back inside the house, which would feel a little empty. My mother would cry, and we never knew how to cheer her up. And, after all the excitement of Papa and Eva's visit, I'd wonder what I should do now.

And then, suddenly, there would be a loud noise on our quiet little street – the insistent blaring of a horn. We'd run out on the front porch, and there it would be – Papa's car, heading down the street, horn blowing all the way, with Papa and Eva calling to us from the open car windows. They'd turn around by the chain-link fence, come back up the street, and drive away again, with us waving and cheering and laughing.

We'd go back inside, in better spirits. I'd get an idea of something good to do, and life would maybe begin to get back to normal. And then, again, that car horn! Beep, beep, beep, beep! We'd run back to the porch, wave and laugh and shout at another return of Papa and Eva.

And maybe again.

But eventually, the car horn concerts would stop, and Papa and Eva would truly have left.

Some years they would come back and drive off again four or five times before they really set off on their way home. My brothers and I would make guesses – how many times would Papa and Eva drive up and down the street this year?

It was hard to predict.

But however many times it was, they always left us wishing for more.

# 14

# Moving

My family had been planning to move out of the house on Biltmore Street and buy a new house. Mum and Dad took us to look at a lot of houses, and finally they decided on one that we would buy. They were set to close on it in late September of my sixth grade year.

When Papa and Eva visited that summer, we showed them a house that would be our new house, and everyone was excited and liked it; even Eva liked it. I was going to have a bedroom that would be just for me, and I showed it to them.

But a few days before the house would be ours, the seller backed out, and all of a sudden, we had nowhere to live, because our house on Biltmore Street had been promised to a new family, and we didn't know what was going to happen..

Mum and Dad scrambled to find another place for us to live, and they rented a first floor apartment in a two story house in Winthrop. We could live there until the following summer, but then we had to move out, because the owner rented it at higher prices to people who wanted to live by the ocean for the summer.

I had never been to Winthrop, but now I was going to live there for a while. I thought it might be nice to live by the ocean, but not if we had to leave before summer time and who knew where we'd live after that!

It turned out I liked Winthrop. My school was good. I didn't have to wear uniforms anymore, because it was a public school, so I asked Mummy to buy me red dresses, because we never got to wear red in Catholic school. And my new teacher was very nice, and she didn't mind if girls wore nail polish. In fact, she even told a girl in my class that her nails looked pretty!

And there were lots of nice kids at my school. I liked them.

But I didn't know what we'd do when we had to move again!

It turned out that someone was selling a house that was only two blocks away from the house my family was renting. Mum and Dad looked at it, and they liked it. Then Mum called Papa and asked him to come look at it too. So in early December, Papa came to look at the house.

It was a cold day, but no snow. We walked the two blocks to 36 Coral Avenue, and this was the first time I saw the house we might live in. It was painted brown, and there was a narrow driveway beside a big long porch on one side of the house, and on the second floor, we could see a smaller porch with a railing around it.

When we opened the front door, we saw a sun porch inside, and then the parlor with a fireplace. And someone had left a shillelagh by the door!

Papa was busy checking all kinds of things, and going upstairs and downstairs and all over the house, and talking to Mum and Dad.

When we went back outside, Papa walked around the house, and he got tangled in some thorny bushes and scratched one ankle. He called out to Mum, "Evie, you're going to want to take these out or you'll get a nasty scratch!"

But Papa thought it was a good house overall, and my parents decided to buy it.

We moved in a few days after Christmas.

Many years later, my mother told me that Papa had given us the down payment for our house, and without him, we couldn't have bought it.

And the thorny bushes that Papa had warned us about turned out to be pretty red rambling roses, and my mother loved them. Despite Papa's warning, they rambled freely year after year after year.

# 15

# Papa Calls

One very important part of Christmas Day was talking long distance on the phone to Papa, and we'd always say hello to Eva too. My mother went first, and then she'd hand the phone to me and each of my four younger brothers in turn. "Thank him for the money he sent!" she'd whisper. We'd each thank Papa, and tell him what we thought we'd get with that money. And we'd tell him about what Santa brought, how things were going in school, and whatever other odd bits of information might come to mind. Papa always had lots of questions for us.

"How's your arm, Kay?" he asked me during one Christmas morning phone call when I was in junior high.

The question was puzzling. "My arms are fine, Papa."

"Oh?" he said. "Then your broken arm has healed?"

"I didn't have a broken arm, Papa."

"No?" he asked. "I thought you had a broken arm!"

"No, I've never had a broken arm." I wondered who he was confusing me with!

"It's been so long since I've had a letter from you, Kay, I thought for sure you must have broken your arm!"

I could feel my face flushing. "I'm sorry, Papa. I'll write you a letter this week."

"No, it's all right, it's all right. But we always enjoy your letters. We like to hear from you, hear what you're interested in, what's you're doing."

The next day, I sat down to write.

*Dear Papa and Eva,*

*I don't know if you've heard of the strange illness that's spreading all over the whole country, Beatlemania, but I've caught it too. The symptoms are going crazy over the most exciting singing group and loving everything about them. All my friends have that same illness. Some people*

I was right. I did not win the dinner with George Harrison's sister, but Papa and Eva enjoyed my letter anyway, and I was forgiven for not having  broken my arm.

# 16

# Talking to Papa about College

It was the summer before my senior year in high school, and Papa and Eva had come for their annual visit. I loved hearing Papa's stories, and often lingered at the table with him long after my brothers had gone on to other activities. Papa and I were sitting at the kitchen table after lunch one afternoon.

"So," Papa said to me, "you'll be applying for college soon. What are your ideas about where you want to go?"

"I want to go to Brandeis, Papa," I said.

Papa nodded. "Hmmm. Named after a Supreme Court Justice, you know."

"I know."

"Good school. But why Brandeis?"

"My English class in ninth grade had a field trip to their library, and it was a great library! They had so many books, and we went on a tour, and, oh, Papa, it was so nice!"

"Hmmm," Papa said. "You liked the library. The library is important."

"And then this past school year, a different English teacher took some of us to a play at Brandeis. It was very modern, and it was so good, Papa! So, Brandeis is my first choice."

"So you liked the library, and you liked the play. Good. Brandeis is a fine school," Papa said. "Where else will you apply?"

"I haven't decided yet."

"Have you talked with your guidance counselor about college?"

"He called me in to talk about my plans, and he asked me what kind of school I was looking for. I told him I want a co-ed school, and definitely not a religious school. I don't want to go to college with people who are all the same, and all believe the same things."

Papa nodded. "Good thought."

"And I said I want to major in English, so I need a school that's very good in English. He said every place is good for English."

"Damn fool," Papa muttered.

"Then he suggested Emmanuel, Assumption and Anna Maria! All-girl Catholic schools! Exactly what I told him I didn't want! So I told him again I'm not interested in them, and he suggested I look at some college guide books, and we'd talk another time. Then he called me in again a few weeks later, after he saw my SAT scores. He told me I should apply to Radcliffe, Smith and Wellesley – all-girl schools again! And I don't want to go to college with a bunch of spoiled rich kids anyway. I told him I want to go to Brandeis. He said I shouldn't have any trouble getting in, but that I should apply to other schools too. He never makes a good suggestion, though! He's no help at all! So I've been looking at the college guides myself, but I'm not sure where else to apply."

"Well," Papa said, "if you'd like another opinion, for my money, the two best schools in the country right now are Reed College and Clark University. Excellent schools! You couldn't ask for more! If I were applying to college this year, those are the ones I'd apply to."

"Thank you, Papa," I said. "I'll look them up."

When I investigated, it turned out that both Reed and Clark were co-ed schools that were not religiously affiliated, and both sounded like interesting places. So far, so good. But Reed College was on the West Coast, about 3,000 miles from where I lived. What was Papa thinking? I couldn't imagine living so far away from my family! I had never been in an airplane, and it would take days to get there by train! I expected I'd get scholarships to attend college, but I didn't think they'd pay for me to travel all that distance just for a vacation. I'd never be able to come home! Nope. Reed was out of the question.

But Clark University was only fifty miles away. That was a much more reasonable distance. I could come home for weekends and vacations without any difficulty. I didn't even visit the Clark campus to see firsthand what it was like. If it was good enough for Papa, it was good enough for me. And, anyway, I expected I'd end up going to Brandeis. Even my unhelpful guidance counselor agreed that I would certainly get into Brandeis. And Brandeis had that wonderful library!

So I sent off my applications to just two schools – Brandeis and Clark.

Both my application essays were fervent and passionate, as much of my writing was in those days. I don't remember what my focus was for the Clark application, but the essay I wrote for Brandeis centered on some then current events. In what was probably intense purple prose, I expressed my sympathy and support for the students who had seized the student center on the Brandeis campus that January, renaming it Malcolm X University. I explained my horror that

Brandeis had called in the police to remove those students, and suggested that the administration rethink its position and become more receptive to new ideas. I also let them know that I intended always to follow my beliefs, even if it would entail civil disobedience.

My guidance counselor, my teachers and my friends had all assured me I'd get in, no problem. When the notification from Brandeis arrived that spring, it was an unhappy shock. They rejected me.

But Clark did accept me, and with a generous scholarship. It was my second choice, and it was a good choice. After all, Papa had told me he considered Clark to be one of the top two schools in the entire country!

I was a little concerned about the matter of the acceptance deposit guaranteeing my place, which was to be sent in soon after I received my acceptance letter. I hadn't realized that I'd have to pay something up front, and asked my mother if we had enough money on hand to pay it. She assured me it wasn't a problem. And so it was settled: I would go to Clark University in the fall.

It wasn't until many, many years later that my mother told me it was Papa who contributed the deposit so I could enroll at Clark.

# 17

# High School Graduation

My graduation from high school was an important milestone, and Papa flew up from Washington to be there. I must admit, it was not a usual Papa visit, where all attention would be focused on him. This was *my* day.

It was also a very important time for me. I was focused, not on my grandfather, but on my high school friends. We were leaving behind all the times we'd shared together, in school and out, for all those years, and moving on to other experiences. Surely we'd remain friends forever! Surely we'd keep in touch always! Surely there was still a chance that some boy would fall madly in love with me, if not that day, then maybe at the parties that night, or at least during the summer, before we had to go our separate ways to different colleges! Being so in love with someone but having to go to different colleges would be tragic, but, still, significantly better than no one falling in love with me at all.

And, of course, there was the matter of how I looked. Wasn't the dress I was wearing under my graduation robe perfect? Wasn't it great that my hair was just the right length? But why couldn't I ever get rid of those split ends? Did I have to brush my hair every five minutes for it to look all right? Who knew that the graduation cap would be so difficult to keep in place? And which side was the tassel supposed to be on anyway?

There was little time for me to focus on Papa. I was as self-absorbed as any other seventeen-year-old graduating from high school.

My parents, my brothers, Nana Lydon and Papa all came to the graduation, which, from what I recall, went off without a hitch. We took photographs with the high school as a backdrop, and my friends and I had tearful hugs in the school corridors before and after the processional. Then it was back home for us -- dinner, talking, coffee, a cake, our family celebration.

What really interested me, though, was getting back to my friends at the parties that night. I left the house as soon as I possibly could.

I remember the party at Phyllis' house, crowds of us in the living room spilling out onto her front porch, down the stairs, onto the sidewalk. No one drank anything other than the soda her parents provided. No one used any other substances, at least so far as I knew. No one was rowdy.

We talked and talked and laughed, reminiscing, suddenly acutely important to each other in a way I don't think we'd ever been before.

Eventually the party ended, and we broke into smaller groups to walk home, but we didn't really want to go home yet. We wanted to talk. We lived in a town that was a mile and a half square, and I think some of us were intent on walking all of it that night. And we talked -- of college, goals, our beliefs, what was important to us at the core, or, at least as close to the core as we were able to get. As it got later, one or another would drop off and go home. Eventually, three of us were walking the darkened streets: Richie, Anne and me. I don't remember who suggested it, but it was pretty late anyway, and we decided to stay up all night and watch the sun rise over the ocean.

I lived closest to the ocean, so we waited for the sunrise at the beach wall just up the street from my house. We kept talking, until around 5:00 AM, when we finally saw the beautiful colors of the sunrise. Then we walked back down my street. Richie gave me a kiss on the cheek and a hug. Then he and Anne set off for their homes.

My family never locked the doors of our house, so I knew that getting inside wouldn't be a problem. I took off my sandals and tiptoed inside. Most everyone would be asleep, but I was worried about Papa. He was a notorious insomniac who was generally up every day no later than 5:00 AM. What's worse, he'd been assigned a bed in an alcove upstairs through which I had to walk to get to my bedroom. The one time in my whole life I had stayed out all night, and I was probably going to get caught!

I scarcely dared to breathe as I went by the alcove. It was silent. Papa was lying in bed on his side with his back toward me. Was he awake? Would he say something about my having stayed out all night? Would he be angry? Would he tell my mother?

He moved one foot, but he didn't make even the slightest sound.

I went into my room, changed into a nightgown and got into bed.

It seemed I'd only been asleep for a minute when my mother called me. "It's six-thirty, and I'm making bacon and eggs for breakfast. The coffee's ready and Papa's down in the kitchen! Dad will be home soon with doughnuts."

"I'll be right there," I said.

When I came downstairs, my mother was interested in hearing all about the party and who was there. "What time did you get in?" she asked.

I tried to look wide awake as I lied. "Um, I don't know. I didn't look at the clock."

"I didn't even hear you," she said. "Did you wake up when she came in, Papa?"

"Me?" he said. "No, I didn't hear a thing. Slept like a baby all night."

"That's unusual for you, Papa," she said.

"Must be the ocean air," he said.

# 18

# The Summer before College

During that summer after graduation, I had a had my first full-time job at Massachusetts General Hospital, in the kitchens of the Baker Building, from ten in the morning until seven, or earlier if I was quick about it, five days a week with a rotating schedule so I worked every other weekend. My responsibilities were setting up the patients' meal trays with paper placemats and silverware in advance of serving food, next dishing out each plate as instructed by a dietary aid for each patient on my floor; and then cleaning up the kitchen, and afterwards, washing the trays and the dishes returned from the patients' rooms; and starting the whole process all over again to leave things ready for breakfast service. A good portion of my summer was spent in a hot kitchen, standing between a stove with water boiling behind me, and in front of me, a hot truck of food sent up from the main kitchen in the basement of the building.

We were never, never, never to eat any of the food that came upstairs, no matter how much was left after everyone had been served. If the dietitian were to catch one of us kitchen workers sneaking so much as one grape, we would be fired on the spot. I don't know how the year-round employees dealt with that regulation; they didn't say. There were several other girls who were also summer replacement employees, all of us recently graduated from high school, working before starting college in the fall. We would, in pairs, occasionally sneak a cup of chocolate ice cream into the pocket of our uniform aprons and take a bathroom break, giggling from separate stalls inside which we ate our treat, so as not to be caught should a dietitian suddenly enter the Ladies Room.

At the end of my workday, I'd rush up Cambridge Street to the Bowdoin MBTA station, catch the Blue Line train to Orient Heights in East Boston, and take a bus from there to Winthrop. When I got home, I'd dash upstairs, change into my bathing suit, and run up to the beach for a late dip.

I worked hard all summer. During my bus and subway commute, I'd read mostly classics, often Russian novels. At work I had lunch breaks after the patients were finished with their meals. I'd take my sandwich to a crowded waiting area, where I'd watch people and listen to snatches of conversation, which seemed to me an important basis for writing good fiction. And I dreamed of what it would be like to go to college in the fall, soon *please*! I'd be able to pursue my true goals and resume my real identity as a Student, with a capital S, learning about all kinds of important and lofty things.

Late in August, when my summer job was finally over, my mother took me with her by train to Washington, D.C., to visit Papa and Eva. I was so excited! I had never been to Washington before. Other than our trip to Chicago to visit Papa when I was three years old, I didn't remember ever having been out of New England. Now, at last, I was going to see a little more of the world!

My father took us to the train station and carried for us the black and white leather suitcases we had packed for the trip. Dad came aboard with us to put our luggage onto the rack over our seat, and then waited outside the train, waving to us and making faces at me to make me laugh until our train finally departed and Mum and I were on our way.

I was fascinated by all I could see from the train -- the houses and yards, the towns, the cities, the businesses; the winding coast in Connecticut, with a view of swans swimming in one place; the red of the soil in northern New Jersey; the brick, brick, brick buildings in Pennsylvania, the bridges, the billboards, the roads -- it was all new to me, and all thrilling!

My mother and I talked and talked, and, when we were hungry, we went to the train's dining car and ordered lunch. I could watch the miles zoom by as I ate my sandwich and sipped my coffee. It was almost as good as being a character in a book!

When we arrived in Washington, Papa met us. He grabbed the suitcases and ushered us into his big car. "I'll just give you a quick look at the Lincoln Memorial before we head home," he said. "We'll be back here tomorrow, but I want to make sure you get to see it at night. That's the best view of Lincoln. Look at him, the sorrow in his face!"

I looked at everything -- Lincoln's Face, the Memorial, the government buildings, the people on the streets, and the highways and roads we took as Papa drove back home to the second floor apartment in Laurel, Maryland, where Eva had dinner ready for us. We had a wonderful time, even though Eva gave us what seemed to me a very strange salad that had apples and nuts in it. Mum had never made anything like that.

The next day, Papa, my mother and I went on a tour of Washington. Papa was partial to Lincoln and Jefferson, and we toured both those memorials, reading everything there was to read on the walls and plaques. Papa read some of the Jefferson quotations aloud to us. "Amazing man," he said. "Where could we find a man of his caliber in the world today? We couldn't. We just couldn't. What a mind! What courage! What clarity of expression!"

Next we saw Congress, the National Cathedral, the statue of the Marines raising the flag on Iwo Jima, and went to Arlington to see the eternal flame at President Kennedy's gravesite.

I was relieved Eva hadn't come on the tour, because I was a bit wary of her. Every time she came to our house, she always complained about something – the lamps didn't have bright enough bulbs, the broth wasn't thick enough in the stew my mother made, the food was too bland, our thermostat was set too low in cold weather or our weather was too hot and humid in summer, there were too many rocks on the beach, or someone or other wasn't cultured enough. And I couldn't forget that time when she yelled at me because I didn't cry when I fell down and cut my knee. From the way she acted, I thought she liked my mother and my brother John, and I didn't know if she liked my other brothers, but she didn't like Dad, and she didn't seem to like me either. And anyway, she wasn't actually my grandmother. She really was no relation to me at all. But I was always nice to her, and polite, just like I would be to anyone, but nicer to her, really, because she was Papa's wife, and I would never want to hurt Papa's feelings by being mean to Eva, no matter what strange things she came up with, or how much she complained when she was at our house.

And I tried not to complain or be critical at Papa and Eva's. I had never had a salad with apples and walnuts in it, but I smiled and ate it that first night we were there. My eyes may have nearly popped out when I saw the half inch thick layer of brown sugar that Eva used to coat the ham she served us, but I didn't say a word about it.

Other than eating and sightseeing, a prominent activity during our stay was going to the pool at Papa and Eva's apartment complex. We also had get-togethers with a number of their friends. We visited in Silver Spring with a woman Eva had known since childhood. Her name was Betty, and her husband was Lou, and they had four grown up children. We had a wonderful meal outside in their beautiful yard. Unfortunately, they served water melon, which I didn't like, but I ate the whole piece she gave me, just to be polite.

I remember also meeting one of Papa's neighbors when he came by for coffee and cake. Paul was a young man who was finishing up his divinity studies. He and Papa really hit it off well, and Eva doted on him.

"My granddaughter's visiting before going off to college this fall," Papa said.

"College in the fall? Where are you going?" the fellow asked me.

"Clark University," I said.

"Where?" he asked.

"Clark!" I said, a little louder.

"Where is that?"

"Worcester, Massachusetts," I said.

"In Worcester? I've never heard of the school," he said.

"Freud spoke there," I told him.

"Freud?"

"Yes," I said. "The only college in the United States where Freud ever spoke was at Clark."

"In Worcester, you say?"

"Yes, at Clark!"

"He doesn't understand. He thinks you're saying *clock*!" Papa told me.

"I *am* saying Clark, Papa," I replied.

Papa turned to his friend. "It's her Boston accent, Paul. She's saying *Clark*! C-L-A-R-K."

"Oh!" Recognition brightened the fellow's face (and mine). "Clark! That's a great school! I'm sure you'll love it!"

# 19

# Freshman Year of College

I went off to college at Clark University with expectations of great things to come. I believed I was leaving behind any petty cliques in high school and entering a sphere where everyone was accepted and valued. I imagined I'd find myself in an intellectual wonderland in which I'd learn great, new and important ideas, and meet bright, curious fellow students with whom I'd discuss all these exciting concepts. Maybe one of the guys would also fall in love with me? Thus mentally prepared for utopia, I found my first semester at Clark a tough adjustment.

For one thing, I had no idea I'd be homesick. I'd been away from my parents and brothers only a few times in my life. My mother's mother and my father's mother had each taken me to Cape Cod for a few days, but that had been when I was in elementary school. Over the ensuing years, I'd had lots of opportunities to think about how much of a pain it was to have little brothers. Who knew I'd miss them so? My first week at college, in what became my habit, I brought my packed duffel bag with me to my Friday afternoon class, and immediately upon the end of class, I left for the bus station so I could go home for the weekend. And so it went for weeks.

It wasn't just the homesickness.

Some of my classes were pretty disappointing. I had hoped English would be my major, but I couldn't get into the English class I wanted because it was already full, and the English class that I got stuck with instead was dull and uninspiring. My Social Stratification class was dry and boring, and my European history survey class was leaden. Luckily, French was interesting, and my freshman proseminar on the Ancient Origins of Western Civilization was absolutely thrilling.

But socially, I was lost.

Most of the students seemed to be more sophisticated, more cosmopolitan, and definitely more cool than I could ever hope to be. My roommate was from Manhattan, and, although she was a very kind and friendly girl and I liked her, I was in awe of her. Her clothes were perfect, ever so much cooler than mine. Her family lived in a tall building with a doorman. Her bedspread was an Indian cotton print, she tacked the camel picture from a Camel cigarette package on her bulletin board, and she played Procol Harum, Vivaldi's "Four Seasons" and Jimmy Hendrix on her stereo. Her hair was amazing - full, curly, and down to her waist. She already knew lots of other Clark students, who also hailed from "The City."

It was 1969, and no one on campus that I ever met talked of substance abuse; no, they talked of expanding their minds, a process which had absolutely nothing to do with those inspiring classes I'd imagined I'd take, but quite a lot to do with marijuana, hashish and "acid;" unless you were too uptight.

I was too uptight.

I'd never tried drugs, had never wanted to, and my exposure to alcohol was quite limited. I had tasted champagne on New Year's Eve my senior year in high school when my best friend's father allowed us girls to have one glass of champagne to toast with her family on the stroke of midnight. It took only one sip for me to conclude I didn't like champagne, and I didn't finish it. Prior to college, that was my entire experience with alcohol.

Early in the semester, on a Monday morning after a weekend I'd spent at home with my family, one of my roommate's "City" friends sat down with me in the dining hall at breakfast. "I had the most incredible weekend!" she told me. "I tripped with Charlie Witlow, and it was beautiful!"

I sat, eating my toast and drinking my orange juice, as she continued gushing more details. I nodded, I smiled, but inside I was thinking, "I am never, never, never going to have a social life here, because, even if I get over being homesick and manage to stay on campus for an entire weekend, I am never, ever going to trip with anybody!"

And sex. Everyone, it seemed, was sleeping with someone, or had just broken it off, or was about to take up with someone. In principle, I had nothing against sex. But I had never had a boyfriend, never been kissed, other than on the cheek as a friend, never held hands with a boy, never been on a date. No guy had ever seemed in the least bit interested in me, and it didn't look to me like that was about to change anytime soon.

And everyone else knew lots of things that I didn't. But I was determined to learn.

Take S.D.S., for instance – I'd read about them in the newspaper and news magazines. Who, student or not, wouldn't be in favor of a democratic society? Democracy was essential, wasn't it? I'd had great hopes for S.D.S., but those were soon dashed when I attended a student meeting at which some kid reported on the S.D.S. summer convention. It seemed S.D.S. had broken up, splitting into two groups -- the Weather Men (later known as the Weather Underground), who were absolutely nuts, the kid said, and some other people who called themselves S.D.S., but it wasn't at all like the old group, and instead represented a take-over by another group. A lot of people, weren't with either group and had just left. Who knew how we'd ever manage to get the country straightened out? Or how I'd ever manage to be part of it? I was still too homesick to stay at school on the weekend!

I finally managed it the weekend of October 15, the day of the National Moratorium to End the War in Viet Nam. Demonstrations were held all over the country that Saturday, and I decided to participate in the Worcester demonstration against the war.

The Worcester demonstration was huge and I was one little person in the midst of a vast crowd. With hundreds of fellow Clarkies, I marched down Main Street to the rally at City Hall in downtown Worcester.

I called my family on the Sunday of that weekend and told my parents about the antiwar events I'd attended. I knew that there was a national demonstration planned for Washington D.C. on November 15. "They're renting buses to take students there," I told my mother. "I have to go."

"Dad and I will talk about it," she said.

"I'm going," I said, "with, or without, your permission."

My parents were not pleased. For a while, my mother insisted that I could only go to Washington for the demonstration if she went along to protect me.

"How could you protect me? And from what?" I demanded. "This is a peaceful demonstration!"

Eventually, she backed off. When I told her there would be one bus which would deliver demonstrators in Washington for the Saturday march, but would not depart for Worcester until Sunday afternoon, she insisted that I take that one, and stay Saturday night at Papa and Eva's. I agreed. It was arranged that I'd call Papa and Eva from Washington after the demonstration, and they would come to pick me up. I'd spend the night with them, and they'd take me back to D.C. the next day to get my bus. That reassured my parents, at least a little.

Although Papa had taken me to many monuments in Washington just a couple of months before, this trip was much different. This time, I went to Washington without him as a tour guide, instead following along with thousands of other people the route of the march, at times seeing things I recognized from Papa's tour, at other times seeing government buildings which I couldn't identify, but which seemed vaguely familiar. I remember that the vast line of us stalled at one point near the Washington Memorial before beginning to move again. I stayed pretty close to new friends from school.

It was cold on the day of the March, and I had on a scarf, mittens and a winter jacket with a hood. The weather was beautiful, the crowds massive, and the speeches, at least what I could hear of them, inspiring. With all those people there, I thought we must really be making a difference. Someone said that there were a hundred thousand people there, and I was sure they were right, although I had no idea how anyone went about making an accurate estimate of the size of a crowd.

After the demonstration, I wandered around Washington with a few people from Clark. They would all be going back on the Saturday buses, but they had some time to kill and we decided to walk around. I figured I'd call Papa and Eva when it was time for my new friends to go back to the buses.

We were walking along the side of a government building, the entrance to which was around the corner, when abruptly there seemed to be a lot of noise and commotion. I had no idea what was going on. Suddenly my eyes, my nose and my throat were burning, I was coughing, and it was awful to breathe. "Tear gas!" a guy, Bob, from my school shouted. "Come on!" He grabbed my hand, turned, and began running with me away from the building. It was hard to see, and I had no idea where we were going. I just knew we were trying to get away from the tear gas. At one point, we came to an area where there were some stores. A middle-aged woman walked out of a five and ten and began choking and coughing. We didn't seem to be able to escape the tear gas. We kept running. "Here!" Bob said, pulling me into an alley between buildings. "There's a water faucet. Wash your face and hands!" He turned on a spigot on the side of the building, and I crouched and stuck my face under the cold running water. When I had washed, he wrapped my scarf around my face and then washed his own face and hands. "I saw a phone booth up the street at the next corner," he said. You can call your grandparents and get out of here." I followed him. It seemed at last we were out of range of the tear gas.

He waited outside the phone booth while I called. Eva answered the phone. "Eva," I said, "you have to come get me! They've gone crazy in Washington and they're tear gassing us!"

"Well, of all things! Where are you?" Eva asked.

I glanced at the street sign and told Eva the intersection.

"That's not a very good neighborhood," Eva said. "Now, I'll give you directions to someplace else you can walk to, so you can wait in a better neighborhood!"

"I'm not going to walk anywhere! They're tear gassing people! Just a few blocks away, I saw some poor lady walk out of a store and get tear gassed!"

"But it's a bad neighborhood!" Eva said.

"I don't care! There's no tear gas here, so I'm not moving!" I said. "I'll wait for you here!"

"Well, all right," Eva said. "But your Poppa's not home, and I don't want to drive in with all that mess. I'm going to send my friend Betty's daughter, Susan. Maybe you could stay in the phone booth until she gets there. You remember Susan. She was the younger daughter. You met her this summer."

"I remember," I said.

Bob waited with me until Susan arrived, and then went on his way. I was so grateful to him, and also grateful to Susan for coming to retrieve me. I'm sure I raved for most of the drive to Papa and Eva's. When I got to their apartment, I thanked Susan, said a quick hello to Eva and then got into the shower as fast as I could to get the tear gas off my skin and out of my hair. Then I resumed raving about the experience of having been tear gassed.

By that time, Papa had returned home from the track. He listened to my account of the events, occasionally interrupting to shout, "Damn fools!" or "Bastards!" It was clear, though, that Papa was on my side. We had the delicious dinner that Eva had made, along with lots of coffee and an assortment of sweets. I was exhausted from the whole day, so, shortly after dinner, I went for a nap on the daybed in Papa's den. I didn't wake for twelve hours.

That Sunday morning, after I got dressed, we had a delicious meal that Eva had prepared — bacon and eggs, buttered toast that Evan cooked in her broiler, and some sweet buns, as well as lots of good, strong coffee. Papa showed me the Washington Post that he'd picked up that morning. We had some time to talk before I had to leave for my bus back to Worcester. I told Papa and Eva that some of my friends were talking a lot about socialism and about maybe joining a socialist group they knew about.

"Hmmm." Papa nodded. "Churchill said, if you're not a socialist at twenty, you have no heart, but if you're still a socialist at forty, you have no head."

Shortly after, Papa took me back to Washington to get my bus. Loaded down with the lunch Eva had made for me, which was big enough that it could have fed half the bus, I traveled back home to Worcester.

I had changed. I had managed to lick the homesickness problem, and I had begun to make friends at college, friends I could rely on. I had been to my first national demonstration. I had been tear gassed, even though I hadn't done anything wrong, but I had survived.

And I had discovered that, at least a little bit, Papa understood, and, what's more, he was on my side.

# 20

# Papa in His Own Words

*During my years at Clark, I wrote less often to Papa, because I was very busy, though not necessarily with my school work. From his end, Papa kept a written conversation going. He often commented on political news items, and let me know about events and people he found significant or meaningful. Below is an excerpt of one such letter.*

Papa sent me this in the summer of 1970, shortly after the death of Walter Reuther.

Reuther was a truly <u>great</u> man – one of the really unsung heroes of mankind, because so many saw him only as a labor leader; a one-sided man, at best, it was thought.

But from the beginning his interest was in the downtrodden. It took shape with labor, because they <u>were</u> downtrodden. But his interest was in more than mere wages – except as wages could bring a better life, and for <u>all</u>. Now that the nation is divided, more so than when slavery split it in Lincoln's day – and, ironically, brought to that point deliberately by another Republican, Nixon – and with Bobby Kennedy silenced, Reuther alone was fighting to have Martin Luther King and his cause remembered, and pushed forward. Reuther was a very "big" man. I don't believe any list of ten could exclude him and win my approval.

I count it as one of the great moments of my life that I once sat ten or twelve feet away from him to hear him speak. It was more than ten years ago – he talked about automation and what it really meant to man, unless man could make the machine subservient to social ends. He was, as so often, far ahead of his time. And as is true, so often, that is tragic for it means what is said, so often, goes unheard. . . .

Incidentally – your great-grandfather Kenneally had something of Reuther's vision too; it was most ironic that he was married to a woman who had every prejudice that her husband was against – from bigotry to narrow patriotism. (In extenuation, however, it must be said that her motives were basically good – they were not born of meanness, simply ignorance.)

# 21

# Grown Up Now

When I graduated from Clark, I went home and looked for teaching jobs, a job that I hoped I could work at until I figured out what I really wanted to do. Unfortunately, teaching jobs were in short supply that year, at least in New England. Instead, I ended up as a secretary in the theater department of Boston University, and on the side, I studied the Russian language and took an education course as well. After a year of that, I decided at the age of 23 to move to Philadelphia. I got a job at the University of Pennsylvania, and I took courses part-time on the side. My first course was in Modern Art.

After some months, when I began to feel more settled in my move, and more content with my finances, I decided to take a weekend trip to Washington to see Papa and Eva. When I called them to make arrangements, they were very excited. It would be about a two hour ride on the train, and Papa was to pick me up at the train station in Washington. On the appointed Friday, I brought my suitcase to work with me, and headed to the train station when I finished work that day. I loved riding on the train. There was so much to see, occasional conversations with someone sitting next to me, and, of course, I always had a book with me.

When I got off the train, I looked for Papa, and there he was – a short man about five feet tall, with a full head of wavy gleaming white hair. He wore glasses supported by an overly generous nose, which my mother used to say, made several ski jumps. His arms were crossed over his chest, and one hand supported his chin as he scanned the departing passengers.

"Hi, Papa," I said.

"My God!" he responded. "I wouldn't have known you! I would have walked right by!" He hugged me and gave me one of those wet kisses I remembered from my childhood. Then he took my suitcase and we headed to the car.

"Eva's making dinner, and she wants me to get you home in a hurry, so we'll just take a quick drive past the Lincoln Memorial. It's beautiful by daylight, but it's best to see by night." Lincoln was one of Papa's three favorite Presidents (the others were Jefferson and Franklin Roosevelt), and anytime we were in the District together, he always took me to see the Lincoln Memorial, in the evening, if possible, but by daylight if needs be.

After paying our respects to Lincoln, we set off on the drive to Laurel. Papa asked me how things were going with my move to Philadelphia. I told him about my apartment, my job, my class, interspersed with his pointing out what interesting sites could be reached by way of various exits from the Baltimore-Washington Expressway.

When we got to their apartment, Eva, wooden spoon in hand, came hurrying from the kitchen to see me. She was an attractive woman about four feet, ten inches tall, with short dark hair always beautifully coifed, intense red lipstick and an imposing bust. Her legs were thin, but muscular, with tiny feet which pointed outward, probably due to her ballet lessons as a child. Immediately, she embraced me, giving me one of her sloppy wet kisses which I remembered so well from my childhood.

"Just look at her, Eva!" Papa said. "She is the image of her grandmother!" I have been told all my life that I resemble my maternal grandmother Evelyn, Papa's first wife.

"What are you talking about, Pat? She doesn't look a thing like her!" Eva said.

"She doesn't look a thing like her? She's the very image!"

"I don't think she looks a thing like Catherine!" Eva said, citing my paternal grandmother.

"Not Catherine! I'm not talking about Jackie's mother!" Papa's voice was loud and irritated. "She looks like Evelyn! She is the picture of Evelyn at that age!"

"She doesn't look at all like Evie!" Eva protested.

"Not her mother Evie!" Papa roared. "*Her grandmother Evelyn!*"

"Hmph," Eva answered. "*I* certainly don't see it." And they were off into a heated discussion of whether I resembled anyone in the family, and if so, who.

We nevertheless managed to eat the lovely dinner which Eva had prepared - Waldorf Salad, and Swiss steak, followed by lemon chiffon cake and accompanied by coffee, coffee and more coffee. Eva pressed me to have some ice cream too. She also put out a plate of candy and cookies.

"When I was a boy," Papa said, "we lived across the street from a bakery. Sometimes my mother used to get their day-old cookies for us. They were sugar cookies, very plain, very cheap, but, oh, did I love those cookies! I've never had a better cookie in my life!"

"He always says that," Eva told me. "He doesn't know a thing about good cookies! These are very nice cookies, Pat!"

Papa took one, broke it in half, and ate a piece. "Good enough for what they are," he said. "But not like those! Sometimes those cookies were just in pieces. As a special treat, my mother would put them in bowls for my sister and me and pour hot cocoa over them. She'd let us eat that for breakfast! We ate it with a spoon. Now, those were good cookies! I've never had any other cookie as good as those were!"

"Hmmph," Eva said. "I like delicate cookies."

We stayed up late, sitting at the kitchen table, talking and drinking full strength coffee right until we went to bed, with intermittent arguments between Papa and Eva that would erupt and subside.

The next morning, Eva, in dressing gown and slippers, greeted me and posed a question about breakfast. "I'm going to make hot cereal," she said. "Which do you like better? Oatmeal or cream of wheat?"

"Oatmeal," I said.

Eva stamped her foot. "Oh, darn!" she said. "Your Poppa loves oatmeal, and I make it for him all the time, but I like cream of wheat better! If you had said cream of wheat, I could make that for breakfast this morning, but now I have to make oatmeal again."

"Cream of wheat would be fine," I said. "Make the cream of wheat!"

"No, you said you like oatmeal better," Eva said. "If you liked cream of wheat better, you would have said so. Darn! It's always oatmeal!"

Despite my assurances that I would be glad to eat cream of wheat, Eva grumbled throughout preparing the oatmeal, cooking it for a very long time the way Papa liked it. However, after we all had eaten a hearty bowl of hot oatmeal, Eva brought out the second course. "We have some rum buns!" she announced happily, setting a box on the table in front of Papa.

As she got plates for us, Papa opened the box. "What happened to these?" he demanded. I peeked in, and saw five plump buns with generous icing, and a sixth bun without a top half.

"I wasn't hungry enough to eat a whole bun, Pat," Eva said, "so I only took half of one. You know I don't like to overeat!"

"But you took the top half," Papa said.

"That's the part with the icing, Pat, and you know that's the only part I like," she said. "I left the bottom half for anyone else who would want it."

"Who would want the part without icing?" Papa demanded.

"Lots of people don't like very sweet things," Eva said.

"Who?" he demanded. And they were off on an argument.

After breakfast, Papa left for the racetrack, having told me that I needn't come, because I wouldn't enjoy it. "It's too smoky, and you'd get bored," he said, while gathering his racing papers and notes and the lunch which Eva had packed him. Eva announced that while Papa was at the racetrack, she would take me to the Hirschorn Museum. "You took that modern art course," Eva said, "so I'm taking you to a modern art museum."

Pleased with her thoughtfulness, I was excited to see what the Hirschorn offered. As we toured the museum, Eva would comment on the various art pieces. "That is the stupidest looking painting! Whatever were they thinking!" or "Why would anyone ever create anything that looked like that? It's just foolishness!" Long past the point where it would have surprised me, Eva confided, "I just hate modern art! It makes no sense!"

"You know, Eva, I like lots of different kinds of art," I said. "I would have been happy to look at other kinds of art."

"No," she said. "You took that modern art class, and I wanted to take you to a place you'd really enjoy."

When we all had returned home, Eva began to prepare meatloaf for dinner. I offered to help, but she said, "No, you talk with your Poppa! You know, Pat, she understands modern art and told me lots of things about it. Some of it even began to make sense!"

He and I sat at the kitchen table, Papa giving me a rundown on his day at the track, and Eva occasionally interjecting and disagreeing with him. When dinner was ready, I was assigned a seat with my back to the bay window, Eva across from me, and Papa to my right, a small television set opposite Papa. This placed us so that everyone would be in good position to see the evening news while we ate, as was their habit. All conversation stopped so that we could hear the opening story of the evening newscast. The news anchor had barely finished his first sentence when Papa started.

"Did you hear that?" Papa shouted. "Did you hear what he said? Those goddamned sons of bitches in Congress!"

"Be quiet, Pat," Eva said. "I can't hear him."

"Be quiet!" Papa thundered. "She tells me to be quiet! We all have to be quiet!"

"Ssssh!" Eva hissed.

"Ssssh!" Papa echoed. "Now she's shooshing me in my own home!" He appealed to me. "Do you hear that? She's shooshing me! I can't make a sound in my kitchen!"

"Pat, you stop that! We're missing the whole story! Can't you just be quiet?" Eva demanded. "He does this all the time," she told me, "and then I can't even hear the news!"

"Quiet! Quiet!" Papa shouted. "We have to be quiet so Eva can hear the news! Eva wants to hear the news!"

"Ssssh!" she hissed again.

"Ssssh! Sssssh! Ssssh!" Papa imitated, as loudly as he could, finger to his lips. "Eva wants to hear!"

They lapsed into a moment of silence, until Eva heard something she felt called for a remark. "Can you believe that!" she said.

"Quiet! Quiet! Sssssh!" Papa shot back. "You hear all that noise she's making?" he asked me.

"I just said -" she began.

"I thought you wanted to hear the news!" Papa roared. "Quiet!"

Eva turned to me. "He drives me crazy with this," she said. "He's crazy about the news. Do you know what he used to do when Nixon was President?"

"The bastard!" Papa said.

"No," I answered Eva as quietly as possible. Luckily, there was a commercial break, resulting in a temporary truce.

"When Nixon was President, and your Poppa used to get up early in the morning to hear the news -" she began.

"What do you know about it?" Papa asked. "You were asleep!"

"How could I sleep through that?" she demanded. "You woke me up every morning!"

"I'd get up at my usual time," Papa said. "She likes to sleep half the day away!"

"Five o'clock in the morning! He gets up every day at five o'clock in the morning!" she said. "And what did he do when Nixon was President? He'd begin shouting."

"I did," Papa agreed. "Of course I did!"

"'Give me some news!' he'd shout," she said. "And I'd tell him, 'Pat, be quiet, you'll wake the neighbors!'"

"And I'd tell Eva," Papa said, "'I don't care about the G-D neighbors! I want some news! I want to know if that bastard is gone yet!'"

"He was shouting!" Eva said. "At five in the morning! Every day!" She began to giggle.

"It is one of the great satisfactions of my life," Papa said, "that, at least so far, the bastard hasn't outlived me!" Then the commercial break ended. We all resumed watching, and Papa and Eva resumed arguing throughout the entire news broadcast, with each asking me to take sides and declare the other to be the troublemaker.

By the time they returned me to the train station late Sunday afternoon, laden with the sandwiches, hard-boiled eggs and cookies Eva thought I might need for my less than two hour train ride home, I was both stuffed and exhausted.

But, for reasons I didn't fully understand, I was hooked. I couldn't wait to come back!

# 22

# Eva and Betty

"I've invited Betty to join us for dinner tonight," Eva told me the next time I came for a visit. "She's just dying to see you!"

"Now you're in for it," Papa told me.

"Oh, Pat!" Eva said. "Don't listen to him," she said to me. "I've known Betty since I was a child."

"Huddling in the cold!" Papa said.

"What do you mean, Papa?" I asked.

"Oh, Betty was born in Russia," Eva said, as if it were an explanation.

"Yes?" I said.

"Well, they were Jewish," Eva said. "And they were religious about it. And you couldn't do that in Russia. Of course, I've never cared a bit for religion."

"You don't know a thing about religion," Papa said.

"Well, I've never wanted to know a thing about religion, Pat!" Eva said. "My parents were Jewish, Kay, but they didn't get so involved with it as Betty does, and I'm not Jewish at all!"

"Of course you're Jewish, darling," Papa said.

"Don't you start up, Pat! You know I'm not religious!"

"That's not the point," Papa said. "You were born Jewish! You are Jewish like I am Italian."

"That's just nonsense," Eva said. "Being Italian isn't the same at all! It isn't a religion! Being Jewish is a religion, and I'm not religious!"

"Being Jewish is more than a religion," Papa argued.

"Well, not for me it isn't," Eva said. "He's always doing this when he knows darn well that I never have anything to do with religion! Your Poppa and I aren't religious at all."

"Religion has been responsible for most of the wars the world has ever seen. More people have been killed because of religion than the other reasons all put together!" Papa was getting louder.

"Don't you start up with that, Pat!" she said. "He goes on and on about religion all the time!"

"Hmmmph!" Papa said, but he refrained from delivering the rest of the anti-religion tirade which usually followed his saying "Religion has been responsible – ."

"So Betty's family was Jewish," I prompted.

"Yes, Betty's family was Jewish, and they had to flee Russia when she was a little girl," Eva explained. "It was very dangerous!"

"Of course it was dangerous!" Papa said. "She has a tremendous story, and she tells it beautifully. Over the years, I've heard her tell the story many times. But this afternoon, I have an appointment at the track!"

Papa was indeed at the racetrack when Betty arrived that afternoon. A small, trim, fast-moving woman with pretty gray hair, she arrived with a brown paper bag in her hand, passing it to Eva while quickly hugging her.

"I've brought you some tomatoes, Eevie," she said. Betty always addressed Eva as "Eevie", pronouncing the first syllable with a long "e", as she had called her when they were children in Portland, Oregon.

"I already have tomatoes, Betty!" Eva replied.

"Well, now you have more," Betty said. "They're from my garden, and you know Pat liked them when you came for dinner last time."

"I can't use them tonight," Eva said. "I have a tomato that's already cut that we have to use first."

"You use them when you can," Betty said.

"I just hope they don't spoil." Eva sighed. "Now let me get you some coffee. We'll have a little bit of a snack before we have dinner." Eva retrieved a jar from the refrigerator into which she'd poured the leftover coffee from breakfast.

"Just some tea for me, Eevie. And I don't need a snack!" Turning to look at me, Betty said, "And aren't you lovely!"

"Thank you," I said.

"And so thin! Stand up a moment!" Betty instructed.

I stood.

"Look at that, Eevie!" Betty said. "What's your waist measurement?" she demanded of me.

"I don't know," I said.

"You don't know your waist measurement? Well, what size do you wear?" she asked. "You must know that!"

"Size five," I said.

"Five!" she exclaimed. "I wear a seven, and I walk three miles every day! I walked three miles this morning."

"Betty's always walking," Eva commented.

"It keeps you healthy, Eevie," Betty said. "I don't have any breakfast until after I come back from my walk, and then I just have a rice cake.

"They don't have any taste," Eva said. "They're so dry!"

"You want all those sweets, but they're no good for you! I like something light," Betty said. "But imagine! I can hardly believe it! Your granddaughter wears a smaller size than I do! She was a chubby child, wasn't she?"

Eva, meanwhile, was on tiptoe, reaching for some of the Belleek saucers and teacups that she kept on upper shelves of her corner hutch. At five feet one and a half inches, I was the tallest person of the group, so I took the china pieces down and put them on the table. Betty picked up a cup, and then another, turning them over and examining them carefully. "You know, Eevie," she said, "two of these are chipped, and one has a crack. What a shame!"

"Well, I drop them sometimes," Eva said as she began to fill the cups.

"She's so careless," Betty said to me. "You should only use them for special occasions, Eevie!"

"What good would they do me if I didn't use them?" Eva asked.

"But you break them!" Betty answered.

"And if they break, I glue them back together," Eva said. She put a plate of cookies on the table. "Now let's sit down with our snack before I have to start making dinner. Have a cookie, Betty."

"I've already had my lunch, Eevie," Betty said. "You know I don't like to eat between meals, and I don't like to eat all those sweets!"

"One cookie isn't going to hurt you," Eva said, as she stirred saccharine into her coffee.

"Eevie always loved the sweets," Betty told me.

"When I was a girl," Eva said, "there was a little lunch counter near our home, and the owner asked my mother if I'd be willing to work there after school and help them out. They said I could take a meal there when I worked, and they'd pay me too. I was just thrilled! Oh, the pies and the cakes they had there! But after just one week, the owner told my mother that they couldn't afford to keep me working for them, because I ate too much!" She giggled.

"She was a chubby little girl too," Betty said.

"I was," Eva agreed. "I was so sorry to lose that job, because those cakes and pies were just delicious!"

"That's Eevie," Betty told me. "But how is your mother doing, Eevie?"

"She's having a little heart problem," Eva said, "and she insists on seeing the same doctor she's always seen. I told her that she needs to see a top man! Pat and I always go to a top man! But she just continues with that same doctor she's gone to for years. She's set in her ways. Well, you know how she always was."

After our snack, Eva explored her tightly packed refrigerator and extracted the meatballs and tomato sauce that she had prepared for the evening meal. She then pulled out the step ladder and began to climb it in order to reach down a pot that she kept on top of her cupboards. Betty watched nervously and then jumped up. "Be careful, Eevie! You're going to fall!" she warned. "She's never careful!"

Relishing another chance to play the tall person, I offered to get the pot, but Eva pooh-poohed the suggestion. "I do this all the time!" she said, as she tottered on the step ladder, barely reaching the pot, and then dropping it onto the kitchen floor.

"And she almost kills herself," Betty added.

When Papa returned from the track, he greeted Betty warmly, and then excused himself so that he could shower and change before dinner. Preparation in the kitchen ratcheted to a higher level, as Eva assigned me to grate cheese we would sprinkle on the pasta.

"What can I do to help?" Betty asked.

"You can help with the salad," Eva said.

"The salad?" Betty sighed. "I always have to make the salad!"

Eva rummaged through the refrigerator again. "Here, Betty," she said, handing her a piece of onion covered with plastic wrap. "You can slice the onion for the salad."

"The onion," Betty echoed as she opened the wrap. Meanwhile, Eva added a heaping tablespoon of sugar to the tomato sauce, and I commenced grating. In the background, I could hear the sound of the shower.

"What kind of cheese is this?" I asked.

"Fontina," Eva said. "I always use Fontina for grating."

"Fontina?" Betty asked. "Not parmesan?"

"Pat loves Fontina! He usually grates it for me."

"Fontina," Betty murmured.

"It's what real Italians use," Eva claimed.

"Eevie!" Betty exclaimed. "What have you done to this onion?"

"What do you mean?" Eva said.

"I have never seen anyone cut an onion the way this onion is cut! Look at that!" Betty said, showing me about a third of an onion that had been cut lengthwise. "How can I possibly slice something like this for a salad?"

"What do you mean?" Eva asked. "Of course you can slice it! It's very easy!"

"How? How can I possibly make reasonable slices for a salad?" she asked Eva, and then, in a quieter voice, said to me, "This is just the way she is! Who else would ever slice an onion this way? Have you ever seen such a thing?"

With much heated commentary back and forth, Eva and Betty argued through the cutting of the onion, each totally exasperated with the other, and proceeded to a debate on the best amount of tomato for the salad, and whether or not salad dressing should contain sugar, and if so, how much. Finally Papa, freshly showered, returned to preside over dinner. Since Betty was an honored guest, we ate dinner that evening without the usual ritual of watching and arguing over the evening news. Papa was positively gallant, praising the food, delighting in the slices of Betty's tomato that had, after all, made it into his salad, asking Betty about her children and grandchildren, and also entertaining us with anecdotes from his afternoon at the racetrack. The quibbling between Eva and her lifelong friend subsided.

After Betty left that evening, we returned to the kitchen table as usual for an evening snack, this time consisting of coffee, ice cream, and another slice of the cake Eva had made.

"So now you've heard Betty's story," Papa said.

"No, Papa," I said. "She didn't mention it."

"Didn't mention it?" Papa said. "That's a surprise!"

"You'll hear it next time, I'm sure," Eva said.

On a number of occasions following that day, I would listen to Betty and Eva quibble about the choice, preparation and serving of food. I would hear them talk of children and grandchildren, what plays they had seen, what books they had read, and the best way to do any number of things. My own children would one day hear them debate the proper way to slice strawberries to be served over ice cream and angel food cake.

But, sadly, I never did get to hear Betty tell of her escape from Russia.

# 23

# Eva's Mother

Eva's 82-year-old mother Lena had been widowed for about three years and was suffering health problems when she came from Portland, Oregon to stay for a while with her daughter and son-in-law. To accommodate her needs, Papa and Eva moved from the upstairs apartment to a larger apartment on the ground level of their building, and Mother, a thin, pale, quiet woman, took up residence in the guest room. I think she lived with them less than a year, and I visited only a couple of times during her stay with them.

At breakfast on one Saturday morning when I was visiting, Eva announced her game plan for the day. "I'm taking Mother to the pet store this morning. Mother has always loved birds!"

"Parakeets." Mother's soft voice had a hint of an accent. "They make happy little sounds and talk to me. I always had a parakeet at home."

"You'll have a parakeet here, Mother," Papa said, patting her hand. She smiled. "What will you call it?"

"I'll call him Pete," she said.

"Pete! You always call them the same thing," Eva said. "Every bird you've ever had was named Pete!"

"I'll see Pete this afternoon when you bring him home," Papa said to Mother. "You have a good time picking out your parakeet!"

"You can stay here and keep your Poppa company," Eva told me. "He's not going to the track today."

A few hours later, Eva and Mother returned with a large cage, mirror, toys, food, and a shiny black bird a little larger than a cockatiel.

"Where's the parakeet?" Papa asked.

"Not a parakeet," Mother said. "We didn't get a parakeet."

"This one is much more interesting and exotic," Eva said.

"What is it?" I asked.

"A toucan," Eva answered.

"That's not a toucan!" Papa said.

"It is too, Pat!" Eva said. "You don't know anything about it!"

"Darling, a toucan has a big beak with bright colors on it!" Papa said. "That's not a toucan!"

"This is a different rare kind of a toucan," she said.

"Goddammit!" Papa said. "What happened to Mother's parakeet?"

"A parakeet is such an ordinary bird, Pat," Eva said. "Mother will like Papeeto much better."

"Papeeto!" Papa said. "I thought Mother wanted to name the bird Pete!"

"Pete is such a common name," Eva said. "Papeeto is similar, but it's a much more sophisticated name! It fits him!"

Mother didn't complain that she hadn't been able to get the bird she wanted, or to name it what she wanted to call it. If Eva preferred the big black bird, that was all right with Mother. She didn't even mention that Papeeto didn't chirp cheerily, but instead let out an occasional loud squawk.

Nor did she complain a few weeks later when Papeeto began to lay eggs, and was renamed Papeeta.

# 24

## Guests to Dinner

"Norm and Paul are coming for dinner tonight," Eva told me at breakfast one Saturday when I visited. "You remember Norm and Paul!"

"I think I remember Paul," I said. "Was Paul the young man who lived down the hall that time I visited before I went to college?" I asked.

"That's him," Papa said.

"Well, he hasn't lived in the building for years," Eva said. "He moved out a long time ago! I can't believe you remember Paul from way back then!"

"Didn't he have something to do with religion?" I asked.

"That's him," Papa said. "He's a minister."

"Don't you start up, Pat," Eva warned.

"What? What? What?" Papa said. "What did I say?"

"Don't you get started on religion again! You drive me crazy with that stuff!" she said. "And don't you bother Paul tonight!"

"Bother him? Don't pay any attention to her," Papa advised me. "Paul and I are good friends. We enjoy good discussion."

"Your Poppa's always pestering him about religion," Eva said.

"Pestering him! You don't know what you're talking about, Eva!" Papa said.

"I told you not to start up with me, Pat," Eva warned. "I have too much to do today. I have to make a chiffon cake!"

"A chiffon cake!" Papa said. "Paul will like that!" He laughed.

Eva shared a conspiratory giggle. "Paul loves his sweets!" she told me. "He always says he's dieting, but when I bring out the dessert, he just can't help himself!"

"Watch him," Papa said. "He'll tell you he has to watch his weight, and then he'll have a piece of cake, and the next thing you know, he's running his finger along the cake plate to get another dab of the icing!"

Later, while Eva got washed and dressed, a process that generally took at least two hours, Papa and I sat at the kitchen table drinking coffee and talking.

"My father hated religion," he said. "Wouldn't have anything to do with it! But my mother was another story. She was a devout Catholic. My father forbade her to step even one foot into a church. She used to take me downtown in Boston and we'd duck into a church so she could go to go to Mass. I was just a little boy. 'Don't tell your father,' she'd say. She used to bribe me, taking me out for hot cocoa and cookies on the way home. I'd swear I wouldn't say anything, but I always told him, every time." He shook his head.

"When she died," he continued, "my father wouldn't go into the church for her funeral. He stood outside and waited until the service was over, and then he went along to the cemetery. He loved her; he wore a black armband for a year. We all did. But he hated religion!

"My mother's brother back in Italy was a priest. When she came to this country, she left my brother Guido in her brother's care so Guido could become a priest too, but Guido had an eye for the girls. Finally Uncle the Priest had to admit that Guido would never make a priest, and so Uncle the Priest sent him to America. Guido lived with us until he and Aurelia married."

When Eva returned from her ablutions, she spent the afternoon baking and cooking and talking, nibbling, and drinking tea and coffee. I helped out when permitted.

That evening, Norm and Paul arrived around 6:00, bringing along a small shopping bag. Eva answered the door with a wooden spoon in hand. Paul was only eight years older than I. He was slim, with brown hair and glasses, and he moved and talked quickly and with animation. Norm looked maybe a little older than Paul, with some silver mixing in with his dark hair. He was soft spoken and slower moving. They were both very warm, kind people. After introductions, we gathered at the kitchen table. Paul announced, "We brought you something from Bermuda, Eva."

Eva put her wooden spoon down and sat with us. "Oh, Paul!" she said, smiling, "you didn't have to do that!"

"With the duty-free shop, we couldn't resist," Norm said. "I picked it out."

Eva's face glowed with excitement. She pulled the ribbon from the package they had placed before her. As she unwrapped a Beleek cup and saucer with a delicate shamrock pattern, she began to cry. "Oh, isn't it just darling!" she said.

"I knew you'd like it," Paul said.

"Stop crying, darling," Papa commanded.

"Oh, Pat, you know I'm sensitive," she said. "It's just that it's so beautiful, and I'm so happy."

"So beautiful, so happy, and what does she do? She cries," Papa said. "What we need around here is some news. So what news can you give us?" he asked his guests.

"We had a wonderful trip," Norm said.

"I ate too much," Paul said.

"I made a lemon chiffon cake," added Eva, who was mostly recovered from her tears.

"I love your lemon chiffon!" Paul moaned. "I'll just have a small piece."

"You said you didn't want to eat too much," Norm commented.

"Now don't you two start arguing about the lemon chiffon!" Eva said. "Norm, did you notice the new backdrop I put over the counter top?" Norm got up to inspect, and he and Eva began to talk together.

"Paul," Papa said, "I have a question for you."

"What is it, Pat?" Paul asked.

"I want to know," Papa said, dragging out each word, "I want to know, how do you explain the existence of evil in the world?" The way Papa said it, this was not a question, but an inquisition.

"Oh, Pat, not that!" Paul said.

"I want to know!" Papa insisted. "How do you explain evil, and how do you explain death? How does your God explain that?"

"Pat, no one wants to talk about that," Eva said.

"Another time, Pat," Paul said. "That's too heavy a conversation for tonight."

Papa, like a tenacious bull dog, would not let go of the nature of evil. "I want to know!" he boomed. Eventually Paul acquiesced. As they debated metaphysics, and Eva told Norm about her backdrop on the countertop, I listened to bits of both conversations. Eva abruptly interrupted Papa.

"Pat, I told you not to bother Paul with religion tonight," she said. "Now I'm going to get dinner on the table! Talk about something else!"

"Talk about something else!" Papa muttered loudly.

"Can I help you, Eva?" Paul asked hopefully.

"No, I have everything ready." Eva winced as she grabbed a hot pot lid with her bare hand.

"Be careful, darling!" Papa said.

"I'm perfectly fine. I'll just have to take the salad out." She stuck a finger in her mouth. I started to the refrigerator to get the salad. "No, no, I'll get the salad," she told me. "You get the salad plates from the top shelf!"

"I'll get them," Paul said, reaching above my head for them.

Eventually, it all worked out, and we sat down to a delicious dinner during which Eva, as usual, did her best to overstuff us. We had some absolutely normal conversation, interspersed with Eva and Papa contradicting each other. As predicted, Paul found an extra dab of frosting on the cake plate and made short work of it.

After a pleasant evening with much dessert, and even more coffee, Norm and Paul went home.

"Wasn't that fun!" Eva said. "Norm and those faces he makes!"

"Paul and his diets!" Papa commented.

Eva smiled. "Your Poppa and I get such a kick out of them! They are such good people, and such characters!"

# 25

## Birth, Death and Names

One Saturday, when Eva called him for lunch, Papa emerged from his den grumbling, "They're asking for it again!"

"What are you talking about, Pat?" Eva asked.

"I have to fill out another damn form! I don't know how many times I've sent in the information, and the next time, they ask for it again!"

"Who asks for information?" Eva demanded.

"The bank, darling, the bank!"

"Oh! We've added a codicil to our will," Eva told me. "The man from the bank was out to see us about it last week. I don't know what you're shouting about, Pat! He was very nice."

"He's nice, he's nice, he's nice! But that has nothing to do with it, darling," Papa said. "No matter how nice he is, I can't give him my birth certificate!"

"Why, Papa?" I piped up.

"He doesn't have one," Eva said.

"I was born at home. That wasn't unusual in those days," Papa said. "And at first they couldn't get me to nurse. I wouldn't take milk, and the doctor didn't think I'd survive my first night. My mother was recovering from the birth, and my father stayed up with me all that night. He said, 'If you're going to leave this world, little one, at least you can go out happy.' To soothe me, he took a hard crust of bread and dipped it in wine, and put it to my mouth. And he kept dipping the bread and putting it to my mouth, and I sucked on it and sucked on it, and I made it through the night. I got past the crisis. But no one ever notified whoever needed to be told in order to get my birth recorded. Any time I've been called upon to present a birth certificate, I have a problem. I'm not even certain of my date of birth. My family celebrated my birthday on January 7, so I take that as my birthday, and because of how old I believed I was when I started school, I say I was born in 1904. But when I've looked for records, all I could find was a baptismal certificate from Sacred Heart Church in Malden for 1905, which would mean I wasn't baptized until I was a year old. So I've never been sure."

"Your Poppa is almost nine years older than I am," Eva said, handing me a platter to put on the table.

"What does that matter, darling?" Papa asked.

"Well, I'm just telling Kay. She might not have known!"

"I'm older. There, now you know!" Papa told me.

"Oh, Pat, don't be silly about it!" Eva said.

"Hmmmph!" Papa stared down his nose at Eva. Turning to me, he continued, "And I don't know why my parents named me Armando. So far as I know, there was no one in the family by that name. For my middle name I use Ralph, but it was originally Raphael, and that was for Uncle the Priest, my mother's brother."

"Pat, sit down!" Eva said. "I'm trying to put lunch on the table!"

"Sit down, sit down!" Papa lifted his arms over his head and made a series of exaggerated bows. "Your wish is my command!"

"He always does this," Eva remarked.

Papa took his seat and looked over the luncheon selection of cold meat loaf, ham, sliced tomatoes, bread and a variety of condiments. "I'm sitting," he announced.

After dessert, Eva went out on an errand, first warning Papa, "Now don't talk her ear off, Pat!" Papa and I stayed at the table, drinking still more coffee, and he resumed his story. "When she first came to this country, my mother asked a neighbor woman what American children eat for breakfast. They have oatmeal and cocoa,' the woman told her. And that's what my mother gave my younger sister Algesa and me for breakfast, almost every single day. My father wasn't happy about it. He told my mother, 'I didn't come to this country so that my children could eat something that in Italy I would give only to a horse!' But she prevailed when she told him it's what American children eat. My parents wanted their children to be Americans. They spoke Italian at home, but they insisted that we children always speak English, so we would be fluent in English, and so they would learn from us.

"Of course, my father had to use English in his work at the hat shop in Boston. My father bought the place, name and all, which is why it was called Kelly the Hatter. He kept the name, because at that time, an Irish name was more acceptable in Boston than an Italian one.

"My father rode a trolley to work every day. In the winter, if there was snow, my mother sent me with a bucket of ashes to meet him at the trolley stop. He insisted that I run ahead of him sprinkling ashes on the sidewalk in front of him so that he wouldn't fall on his way home from work. I had to run backwards in front of him. It made me so angry to have to do that!

"We clashed, my father and I. He was a stubborn man, and he didn't bend.

"My father loved fish, and we often had fish for dinner. I can't stand the stuff! Never could! Every time we had fish for dinner, I'd refuse to eat it. Well, my father wasn't going to have that! 'Up to your room for the night, and no supper,' he'd tell me. My mother would watch me sadly as I left the table, although she couldn't say a thing. But after dinner, behind my father's back, she'd sneak upstairs and bring me something to eat.

"The night my mother died, my father sent me to get the doctor because we didn't have a telephone. I was 13 then. It was winter, and I ran through the crunching snow, repeating over and over the message my father had told me to give to the doctor, 'Mama is dying, please come at once, Mama is dying, please come at once!'

"It was gall bladder. Now they can take care of it; surgery, rest in the hospital, she would have been fine. But then, the doctor couldn't do anything, and she died.

"But before she died, she said to my father, 'Take care of the little one for me.' You might think she meant my sister Algesa, because she was the youngest, but that isn't who my mother was speaking of. No, she knew my father would take care of my sister. Algesa was his favorite. Mama was speaking in Italian, and she used the masculine ending. She was asking my father to take care of me." He shook his head.

"We wore black for a year.

"Maybe 10, 15 years ago, I looked up a favorite old teacher of mine and discovered she was still living. When I telephoned her, she said to me, 'I remember you. You were the boy in black who always wore a black armband.'

"After my mother died, I was so angry with the world that I wanted to fight everyone! There was a field in Malden where the young toughs used to go to box with each other every Saturday. I took up boxing, and I was there every week. In those days, people fought people only of their own race. White people fought white people, black people fought black people. Hell, I didn't care what color anyone was! I was mad at life, and I just wanted to hit someone! There was a professional boxer of the time, Patty, I don't remember the last name, and he was so hungry, he'd cross the color line to fight any taker. That's exactly what I did. I'd fight anyone! The other kids began to call me Patty after that boxer, and that's how I got the name."

We heard the door open, and Eva bustled into the kitchen with a bag of groceries. "You're still at the table! Pat, I hope you didn't talk her ear off!"

# 26

# Letter from Papa and Eva

*When I started graduate school, at first part-time along with a full-time job, and then full-time study along with part-time applied work, my visits with Papa and Eva were less frequent. I had written Papa a long letter about my impressions after having begun full-time study. He responded, and Eva sent comments too.*

10/16/76

Dear Kay –

When you keep your promise about writing, you sure do – and then some. But don't get me wrong, I found your letter very interesting.

I'd make some suggestions – not as a counselor (for as such I was essentially "non-directive" but within a Rankian framework – and sometimes, and only sometimes, a further dash of eclecticism; puzzle that one out if you will!) but as an advisor. The first is that you do all your graduate work at <u>one</u> school, if you are going after a doctorate. It is very rare that a graduate student can go from one school to another without some real loss of time (as well as duplication of effort).

As to the matter of a Ph.D. vs. an Ed.D., pursue the former. The difference is a pragmatic one, a difference existent in the "real" world. As a matter of competence, I don't believe there is ground for the difference, for a student could be as competent a counselor with the one degree as with the other. I might pursue this thought further, but won't. What is important, however, is that the Ph.D. is more prestigious, especially if one is to work in a college or university. Thus, the reference above to the "real" world.

The last suggestion is to settle on your dissertation topic as soon as possible. The reason again is pragmatic. An early choice makes it possible for every course – whether required or elective – contribute maximally to your dissertation. A late choice may mean taking additional courses – either because you would find them necessary to the development of your dissertation or because your advisor (or your "committee") would "suggest" added courses before giving "approval" etc. (I've known of candidates who were hung up an added year or two because of postponing choice of dissertation.)

In the final analysis – however – what you may want to consider most of all is what <u>you</u> want to do. I used to pose it as a trilogy – work with what: things, ideas, people? What will contribute most to whatever your choice is? Courses – for ideas? Practicum – for people? (I rule out things –

70

because I can't see your choice there!) Or what combination would allow both options before making final choice?

Enough for now.

I don't know how deep your interest in testing is. At one time I did quite a bit of work in the area. I still have some books around relating to testing – none of which are new, but still somewhat solid. I'd be glad to send them to you – but if you found they met none of your needs I'd want you to see that they'd end in either a library or with someone who could use them or want them. (I've always had a kind of reverence for books – they are sort of people, I suppose, in my mind! You wouldn't suspect that, would you?)... Some years ago I gave quite a few of my books to Susan [Betty's daughter] because she, too, has a feeling about books.

And before I close, let me add – if need be – that it goes without saying that Eva also – very much so – has that feeling about books. And Eva may want to add a note to this before I send it on. So I'll close here, but stressing three things first -- liked hearing from you, don't wait so long before writing again, and feel free to disregard whatever I've written!

Love,

Papa

(Over)

From Eva

I wanted to add, Kay, that I, too, found your letter very interesting in that you conveyed some of your thinking that for me evolved into many multiple complexes of ideas, planning, feelings, projections – all that precious value of an awe of a particular individual – you! You are so verbal, and this quality in anyone always intrigues me. Your mom has that quality too.

[Papa and Eva had visited my family in Massachusetts earlier that month.] We enjoyed being with them so much and did wish you were there. We picked [your brother] John up in Cambridge the eve of his birthday at about 11:30 p.m. and after returning to your mom's talked with him till 2:30 a.m. or more. He, too, has so much to offer – each of your family in his own interesting way. I hope you will, or have found an apt. by now without bugs. The poor dears do have to live but for pete sake not at Kay Lydon's! The best of luck, and we do look forward to hearing from you and certainly would like you to come visit. Maybe you and John could get together on a time when you could come together. I'd love that. Bye for now.

Lovingly,

Eva

# 27

## Compliments

Papa did not easily pay compliments.

Some weekends when I visited, there were plans for an event which called for dressing up. Eva would emerge from her preparations in a lovely outfit, her hair and make-up perfect.

"Hmmmph!" Papa would say.

"Don't start, Pat!"

"I don't know why women decorate themselves with war paint!"

"He always does this!" Eva would tell me.

"Darling, you look like you've painted a gash in your face!"

"Just stop it, Pat!"

"It's jarring," he'd continue. "Jarring!"

I didn't look to him for compliments that were unlikely to come. Instead, though, I often tried to entertain Papa with stories he might find amusing. If I could get Papa to laugh, that was enough.

Papa was particularly interested in my graduate study in psychology.

"What's the news?" he'd ask.

On one visit, I had an interesting story to tell him.

"I have this one professor who's pretty old school. People say he doesn't like having to teach statistics to female students. But, I need the course, and he's the one teaching it. So this week, he was lecturing, and he put an elaborate series of equations on the board. He gestured toward them and said, 'This is something that only those of you who've studied calculus will understand, so the rest of you just sit this out!' Then he asked a question about those equations. Two hands went up – one from a real bright guy in the class, and one was mine. The professor called on me first, and I gave my explanation. The professor didn't say a word. Not yes, not no, you're right, you're wrong

– nothing. He turned and called on the other student. The guy said, 'I was going to say pretty much what she's already said.' And then he summarized what I had said. The professor said, 'Bob is exactly right!' He went on to expound on how brilliant Bob's point was, ignoring that I had said anything."

"It's a damn shame," Papa said. "You will never get the credit you deserve because you're a woman."

"It's just that one professor, Papa. Other than that, there's no problem."

"You have no idea what you're talking about," Papa said. "Mark my words. Men will never give you the credit you deserve."

# 28

# Lessons in Psychology

Papa surprised me one evening after dinner by lugging a large box of books into the kitchen where we were sitting with our evening coffee. "I thought you may like to take my psychology books back with you when you go. I don't use them anymore. I already gave some of them away, but there are a lot left."

As I looked through the box, I was surprised to find earlier editions of texts I used in my classes, many classics in the psychoanalytic field, a set of Rorschach cards and books on testing, intelligence, development. It was a treasure trove, and I wanted them all! "Thank you, Papa!" I said. "You know, until that letter you sent me, I didn't know you'd been a psychologist!"

"Didn't know I was a psychologist!" Papa exclaimed. "What did you think I did for a living?"

"Mum never told us anything about psychology. She always said you were an English professor," I answered. "If I made a grammatical mistake, she'd say, 'I can't believe that *you, the granddaughter of an English professor,* would say something like that!'"

"Well, I *was* an English professor in Buffalo for ten years or so. I did my graduate work for the doctorate in those years, but didn't work as a psychologist there."

"I didn't know that, Papa," I said.

"When your mother was born in '31, I was teaching English at Canisius College in Buffalo. Me, who's never had any use for religion! Teaching at a Catholic college!" He shook his head. "I've always hated religion! But that's where I was working when I began studying for the doctorate. For over a year, our dining room table was covered with books and papers for my dissertation. Didn't your mother ever tell you that?"

"She did, but I thought your doctorate was in English," I said.

"Hell, no," Papa said. "I wanted to go into psychology, and I began to study at the University of Buffalo. Canisius didn't like that at all! 'Professor Carli,' they said, 'that's a radical place! You don't really want to go there!' They were right that I didn't want to study at Buffalo! I wanted to go to the University of Chicago, which was much more radical! That was the place to be! It was a hotbed of intellectual activity! But, here I was, a married man with a wife and two young children, earning a living by teaching at a Catholic college in Buffalo. I was stuck where I was. So I got my doctorate from the University of Buffalo. I used to get practice in administering tests by giving them to your mother and your uncle."

"I didn't know that," I said. "But when you left Canisius, you didn't become a psychologist then, did you?"

"No," Papa said. "I thought I'd open a rare books store in Boston, but I couldn't make a go of it and I had to look for something else. As a young man, I had wanted to go to Annapolis, but I was too short, so they wouldn't take me. After Pearl Harbor, I thought with such a demand for manpower, I'd get around the height requirement. I tried to get a naval commission, but again, I wasn't tall enough. Instead I got a position with the U.S.O. I traveled around the country setting up U.S.O. centers. We stayed a year in Indiana at the center I opened in Vincennes, and then I went alone to work for the U.S.O. in Brazil for a year. But after that I took a job at the Veterans Administration."

"What did you do there?" I asked.

"I did some testing, and I counseled soldiers who were returning from the war. Ha!" He chuckled, looked down, and folded this arms over his chest. "I applied my psychological knowledge!"

There was clearly a story. "Yes?" I prompted.

He adjusted his glasses. "Well, one time I was seeing a young fellow in therapy. He had been injured in the war and he was recovering, but they were worried about depression. They sent him to me late one afternoon. I had a nice little office, a window near my desk that looked out on the lawn, a comfortable chair opposite the desk for the patient to sit in. So I invite the fellow to sit down, and I sit with my back to the window. I begin the interview, pepper him with questions, but I can't get much from him. Very quiet boy, short answers, even keel no matter what we're talking about. But the strange thing about him was that all the time we're talking, he's holding a thumb up, you know, the way an artist holds a thumb up when he's doing a painting. The whole session, he's got that one thumb in the air. I'm wondering, what does that mean to him? What's he trying to convey? Is he delusional? Is this a symbol of something in his unconscious? I'm baffled; I can't get a grasp of what's going on with him. Finally, our time's almost up, and I can't stand it any longer. It goes against all my training, but I just have to say something!

"'Why do you hold your thumb up like that?' I ask and I wait to discover the deep psychological meaning."

"'Oh,' the fellow says, 'I'm blocking out the sun. It was in my eyes.'"

"I turned and looked out the window at the setting sun, and I held up my thumb. He was right! A thumb was the perfect size to block out the sun! Damn fool that I was, I sat for an hour wondering what he meant with that thumb, and all I had to do was ask!"

"You know," Papa told me the next morning as we sat in the kitchen drinking coffee yet again, "I went into therapy myself once."

"Did you, Papa?" I asked.

"Oh, yes." He leaned back and closed his eyes to tell the story. "Back when you were in high school, I don't know if you remember it, but I had gall bladder surgery."

"That's when you stopped smoking, isn't it, Papa?"

"Yep, yep," Papa said. "I wasn't allowed to smoke in the hospital, and when I was finally discharged, I didn't start again. I thought it might help me. The thing is, before the gall bladder problem, I had never been sick a day in my life! Other people got sick, but I never even caught cold! Not a headache, not an upset stomach, nothing! And suddenly, I was in the hospital, feeling absolutely terrible, having surgery! Little by little, I got better, and I came home from the hospital, and I went back to work, but I wasn't the same person. I was depressed. I couldn't accept the idea that I too could get sick. It seemed to me that somehow I had become old, and it would be all downhill from there; I just couldn't get past it. So I ended up seeing an analyst. She had an excellent reputation, quite well known. We knew each other from professional associations we both belonged to. I made an appointment and I went to see her, week after week after week, but I couldn't shake it. I was still depressed.

"Finally, one session, she said to me, 'The problem is this: you're up against a brick wall, and you keep banging your head against that wall, as if you could knock it down. Your head hurts, and still you keep banging it. And you're going to keep banging your head against that wall until you finally accept that there's nothing you can do to knock it down.'"

"Did that help?" I asked.

"Hell, no!" Papa said. "I was so angry! I said to her, 'I come in every week, and you're not doing a damn thing to help me! You keep me coming back just for the money I pay you!'" He opened his eyes and tilted his head to the side. "That's what I said. Me, a psychologist; I told her she was keeping me in treatment just for the money!"

"How did she react?" I asked.

"She said to me, well, she always called me by my last name," Papa said. "She said to me, 'Carli, there's not enough money in the whole wide world to get me to keep seeing a mean son of a bitch like you for one minute more than you need it!'" He shook his head and smiled. "'A mean son of a bitch,' she called me, and at that point, I turned a corner. I began to see the light at the end of the tunnel!"

# 29

# Bran and Bunnies

"The most terrible thing has happened," Eva told me.

"What?" I asked.

"On Wednesday I went for my regular physical with Kirstner," she told me. "Your Poppa and I both see him, and he's a top man. He insists we have a physical every year!" She took a sip of her coffee.

"But he found a problem?" I was concerned.

"No, he *made* a problem," Eva answered. "He decided to look over my history, and he refused to renew my prescription! It's so crazy! I've been taking it for years and years, and it was never a problem at all! But today I finished the bottle I have, and that's it! No more!"

"What prescription?" So far as I knew, Eva didn't take any medication regularly.

"It's a prescription laxative," Eva said.

"You've been taking a prescription laxative for *years*?"

"I can't even remember when I started taking it, and now suddenly, Kirstner says he won't give it to me anymore! I told him that I'll never be able to go without it! And do you know what he said?"

"What?"

"He told me I don't need medicine at all. He said I should eat bran cereal! Did you ever hear of such a thing!"

"I have, actually," I said. "It sounds like a good idea."

"Hmmmph! I can't imagine that it will be any help!" Eva said. "And have you ever tried bran cereal? I bought a box at the Giant, and I tasted it as soon as I got home. It's dry, and it doesn't taste very nice at all! Starting tomorrow, I have to eat it every day!" She sighed deeply. "I'll probably never go again!"

We spent some time discussing what Eva could add to the cereal to mask its taste, and the next morning, she unhappily ate her bran cereal, which she disguised with half a sliced banana, milk and lots of sugar, making herself finish the whole bowl before she touched so much as a crumb of pastry. To her amazement, the cereal served its purpose, but she continued to dread the prospect of eating bran every morning.

After returning home, I had an idea that might help Eva reconcile herself to her new breakfast regimen. I went shopping and ended up in the aisle for Royal Doulton china.

On my next visit, I arrived on a Friday evening. After another of Eva's delicious dinners, I announced, "I have a surprise for you, Eva!"

"For me?" Eva was wiggling with excitement. "What ever could it be?"

I retrieved the package from my tote bag and presented it. "For you!"

Eva began to cry, as she always did when given a gift. "Oh, Kay!" she said.

"Open it, darling," Papa encouraged.

"Oh, Pat!" She took a deep breath, and began to tear the floral wrapping paper. When she saw the rectangular box, she again began to cry. "Bunnykins!" she said.

"What is it, darling?" Papa asked.

She opened the box and lifted out a small bowl. "Oh, look, Pat!" she cried. "There are little bunnies all over the rim of the bowl, and down at the bottom of it too! Oh, Pat! Look at the little bunnies on the swing! It's so darling!"

"There's a spoon too," I said.

She pulled the child-sized spoon out of a tiny plastic bag. "There's a bunny on the stem of the spoon!" she cried. "It's so sweet!" She grabbed my face and gave me one of those sloppy wet kisses I had dreaded throughout my childhood. "I'm going to use these for my bran every day, and I won't even mind it anymore, because I'll eat it with my little bunny spoon and I'll get to see the little bunnies on the bottom of the bowl as soon as I finish the bran!"

She did use it daily, and although she still grumbled a bit about the dreadful bran, never before or since have a baby bowl and spoon been so loved.

# 30

## Crickets

During a visit I made to my parents' home, my mother was going through a catalogue she had received in the mail. "I don't think I could bring myself to touch something like this!"

"Like what?" I asked.

"It's a stapler shaped like a cricket!" She handed me the open catalogue. "Who in the world would ever want something like that?"

"Eva," I answered.

"Eva?"

"She loves insects," I told my very squeamish mother. "She'd think it was cute."

"She *would!*" My mother shivered at the thought. "Wait! Eva's birthday is next month. Do you really think she'd like something like this?"

My father looked up from the sports page. "Is it expensive?" he asked.

"Well, it's not cheap," my mother said.

"Then she'd like it," Dad said.

"Good! Because I can never think of what to get her!"

On my next visit to Laurel, Eva excitedly displayed the cricket stapler my mother had sent. "Isn't it darling? All the detail is perfect!" she said. "Look at that little cricket face! Every time I need to staple something, it makes me smile. Your mother has such wonderful taste!"

The following summer, my mother took a train to Philadelphia, and I picked her up and drove her to Laurel, where we visited with Papa and Eva for the weekend. Eva was thrilled that my mother at last could see the cricket stapler she'd sent. "I just love it!" Eva said. My mother smiled, but she didn't touch it.

The complications began at dinner that night.

"The salad dressing tastes sweet," my mother commented at dinner.

"I always add a little sugar to it," Eva told her.

"Sugar!" my mother said. "Why would you put sugar in the salad dressing?"

"Everyone does! It brings out the taste."

"You know I'm diabetic, Eva!" my mother said.

"It's just a little bit of sugar, Evie. Your Poppa is pre-diabetic, and it never bothers him."

"I can't have sugar!"

"A little bit of sugar never hurt anyone," Eva retorted.

"Sugar," my mother muttered, pushing her salad aside.

Luckily, Eva wasn't serving ham for dinner. When she prepared ham, she coated it with a thick layer of brown sugar before baking. But Eva had made meatloaf this time, and if my mother could taste the sugar in the tomato sauce covering the meatloaf, she didn't say.

Later that evening, we were sitting around the table drinking coffee and talking when suddenly there was a loud chirp. My mother jumped.

"There! It's back again," Papa said.

"What's back?" my mother asked nervously.

"The cricket," Eva said.

"A cricket? A live cricket in here?" My mother glanced around the room.

"Ever since we moved into this ground floor apartment, we find that crickets sometimes get inside," Papa explained. "Eva usually takes them back outside."

"The other night we heard one, but I couldn't find him," Eva said.

"There it is, darling," Papa called out.

"Where?" Eva demanded.

"Just behind Evie's chair," he said.

Eva peeked under the table, as my mother made a high-pitched squeal and lifted her feet off the floor.

"It's all right, Mum," I said.

"There's absolutely nothing to be afraid of, Evie," Eva said sternly. "It's just a little cricket. Oh, look, Pat! Isn't it sweet?"

"Just keep it away from me!" my mother said through clenched teeth.

"A cricket won't hurt you!" Eva got up from the table and began rummaging in a cupboard.

"Don't let it touch me!" my mother cried.

"Eva will take it out," Papa said, reassuringly.

"Kay, you get under the table and see if you can catch it in this jelly jar," Eva instructed me.

"Me?" I asked.

"You can reach it more easily than I can," she said.

"It's under your plants now, darling," Papa said.

I got on my hands and knees and crawled toward the plant stand. "If I can catch it, how am I supposed to keep it in the jelly jar?" I asked from under the table.

"Just put your hand over the jar!" Eva said.

"I don't want the cricket jumping at my hand," I said. "Get something I can put over the top of the jar."

My mother squealed again.

"I've never seen people make such a fuss over a poor little cricket!" Eva said. "Here's an index card you can hold over the jar when you catch it. But I always use my hand."

Papa, Eva and my mother all watched as I crawled around the kitchen floor in pursuit of the fleeing cricket. Eventually, I cornered it. I nudged him with the index card, but that spooked the cricket, causing him to jump toward my mother, who of course screamed. After a few more of such attempts, I finally caught the little critter, and Eva returned him to the Great Outdoors.

When I returned by myself in early fall for another visit, Papa and Eva reported that there had been several more cricket episodes. That weekend of my visit, though turned out to be quiet; that is, until I got back home.

I had carried everything into my apartment and was in my bedroom unpacking my suitcase when I heard the first chirp -- just one -- loud and high pitched. *Oh, no! Not more crickets!* Had the sound come from the living room? I grabbed a paper cup from the bathroom and went in pursuit. I checked behind and under all the living room furniture, but saw no sign of a cricket. *Well*, I figured, *it'll show up.*

Later, in the kitchen, I heard it again. This time it sounded like it was in the bathroom! I searched there, but, again, no sign of it.

When I was back in my bedroom getting ready for bed, there it was again -- just one chirp. *Maybe in the hall closet?* I wondered, but I couldn't find it, so I went to bed.

I was awakened several times by random chirps, and by 3:00 AM, I had had enough. I was going to find that damn cricket if it took the rest of the night! The sound was coming from just outside my bedroom. It had to be in the hall closet! Well, I'd just empty everything out until I found it! I took out all the sheets and towels from the shelves on the right side of the closet. Nope, not there. I piled the linens on my bed, and proceeded to empty the closet. Not behind the vacuum cleaners. Not in the vacuum cleaners. Not in the wrapping paper. Not in my out-of-season coats. Not in the boots. I dragged a chair from the dining room and stepped up onto it to check the high shelves. Not in the hat box, not in the box of old notebooks, not in the kaleidoscope box. And suddenly, again, a chirp -- a deafening chirp, just outside the closet, right at my ear level, and I was standing on a chair! Was the cricket climbing the walls? I turned in the direction from which the sound had come, and saw it: not a cricket, but the brand-spanking-new smoke alarm that the maintenance crew had installed the previous month. Apparently, they hadn't used new batteries.

At 3:00 AM, it was hard to be good humored about it, but the next night when I called Papa and Eva to tell them about my elusive "cricket," we all had a good laugh.

# 31

# Riding in the Car

I had very clear memories from my childhood of riding in a car which Papa was driving. (The experience of careening down a one-way, one-lane street at 90 miles an hour on a Sunday morning in a densely populated area just isn't easy to forget.) I could also remember my parents talking about an insurance company dropping Papa and Eva's policy because of frequent accidents. Not surprisingly, in adulthood, I was wary of getting into a vehicle which either of them was going to drive. Unfortunately, when I visited Papa and Eva, car rides were often impossible to avoid, because they wanted me to see the sites in the area and spend time getting to enjoy their friends, and they always insisted on doing the driving. I was glad, at least at first, to discover that Papa was no longer the speed demon I remembered from my early years.

One Sunday returning to Laurel after a day at the Smithsonian, I was enjoying Papa's keeping reasonable pace with the other traffic on the Baltimore-Washington Parkway.

"Now, I want to show you something about this next exit," he told me.

"O.K." I noticed that he was slowing a little.

"This is a government site, but there's restricted access," he explained, slowing further.

"That drives your Poppa crazy," Eva said.

I glanced at the speedometer, and noted that it registered in the low 50s. "What do they do there?" I asked.

"That's what I wanted to know," Papa agreed. Now his speed was dropping below 45.

"Papa, the speed limit is 55," I pointed out.

"That doesn't mean you have to go 55," Papa said. "Now I wondered about this place. I just don't like it that the government won't let people see it. So one day I decided to find out about it. "

We were down to 35, and the cars behind us were roaring up and then switching lanes, often uncomfortably close to our bumper. Many made unpleasant gestures as they passed us. "Papa, if we're going this slow, we may get hit," I said, quietly but firmly.

"Let them hit us," Papa said. "So I pulled off on this exit, and almost as soon as I got off the Parkway, I was stopped by a guard."

"You should have seen the guard's face," Eva said and holding, I noted.

Papa continued. "'You can't come in here, sir,' he said to me.

"'Why not?' I asked him. 'I'm an American citizen!'

"'Sir, you'll have to turn around,' he said. And that's all I could get out of him. I couldn't see a damn thing, and he wouldn't tell me a damn thing about the place!"

Eva chuckled.

Having slowly passed the exit and finished his story, Papa again accelerated and I stopped hyperventilating. However, he continued to slow down to what I saw as dangerously low speeds whenever he saw something that merited a look and a story. In local driving, he would even come to a complete stop in the road on occasions when he found something of particular interest.

As the years passed, Papa continued to drive locally. However, he began to leave the highway driving to Eva, who was eight years younger than he, although I was never convinced that made me safer in their car. Papa, in an exercise of gallantry, would always insist when Eva was driving that he would ride in the back seat, enabling me to enjoy the comfort of the more spacious front seat. Kind of him as it was, I found myself thinking of how much closer to the windshield that put my skull.

A complicating factor in going out together in a car was that both Papa and Eva hated seatbelts. Having driven for years before cars came equipped with seatbelts, they didn't take kindly to that new addition. As we were heading out on an excursion during one visit, I reached to buckle my seatbelt.

"You're not going to use a seatbelt!" Eva exclaimed.

"I always do," I said.

"Your Poppa and I never use them," Eva said. "They're really very unsafe!"

"Most dangerous thing in the world," Papa commented.

"They say that seatbelts save lives," I pointed out.

"Maybe a few," Papa grudgingly acknowledged. "But they're going to kill more people than they ever save. They're going to trap people in cars."

"How will people get out if there's a fire?" Eva demanded.

"You unbuckle," I suggested.

"It adds an extra step," Papa said. "And what if the seatbelt jams and the car's on fire? What if the person is unconscious? No, it will just waste valuable time. Seatbelts make car accidents much more dangerous! Much more! I'd never use one!"

"It's very foolish. It makes me very nervous that you're riding in the car with that seatbelt buckled!" Eva told me.

Seatbelts remained an issue of discussion any time we got into the car. Papa would make a comment or two about the danger they presented, and then let the matter drop. Eva, however, got very distressed over my seatbelt use and argued and criticized over it relentlessly. Sometimes when she was driving, I would even, despite great trepidation, go unbuckled to pacify her, provided that it was just local driving. For highways, no matter their objections, I insisted on wearing my seatbelt.

Eva, who was very short, had outfitted her large car to accommodate her small stature. The front seat was moved as far forward as possible, so that she could reach the pedals. She also had a thick wooden plank over the driver's seat, so that she sat high enough to see over the dashboard. She covered the plank with fluffy, ruffled cushions. Thus equipped, she was ready to go, and to go fast. Eva did not believe in letting other drivers get ahead of her. She would zigzag from lane to lane in order to pass the other cars. Still, I would have to say that she spent the bulk of her highway time in the farthest left lane.

One afternoon, as Eva was speeding us along the Beltway, we were witness to a horrible incident. A car well ahead had pulled over on the right into the breakdown lane. Even from the far left lane, we could see the front passenger door open as someone deposited a puppy on grass, and then they sped away. Cars around us began to slow. Eva, who loved all animals, and particularly dogs, came to a complete stop in the far left lane and began to cry.

"Keep going, Eva," I shouted, afraid we'd be hit. "Keep going!"

"Oh, the poor little puppy!" she cried, as cars swerved around us. "How can someone do that?"

"They should be arrested! But you can't stop on the highway, darling," Papa said, "no matter what the bastard did."

"Oh, Pat!" she cried. "The poor little thing!"

Meanwhile, a car on the right pulled into the breakdown lane, stopped, and a kind soul scooped up the poor pup.

"The puppy's all right, Eva," I said.

"It will be hit by a car!" she continued.

"Someone picked it up! Someone has it!" I said. "It's safe!"

"How could someone do that?" she sobbed.

"They've got it, darling," Papa said. "The puppy's safe!"

"Really?" she asked.

"I saw the woman from that green car pick it up!" I said.

Eva breathed one of her deep sighs, wiped her eyes, and resumed speeding down the road.

That summer, Norm and Paul invited us for dinner on a hot Saturday night. Eva, whose size four shoes were a tight fit at the best of times, squeezed her feet into an attractive pair of summer shoes and dressed in bright colors for the occasion. Despite Papa's complaint that red lipstick made anyone look garish, she applied her signature bright red lipstick, daubed on the scent that she mixed herself, and put on earrings too. Papa obligingly changed his shirt, put on fresh khakis, and wore his penny loafers as well as his teeth that evening. Getting into the car, I mentally juggled the prospect of Eva at the wheel, the short local drive and the prospect of a long debate about seatbelts. I decided to skip the argument and live dangerously. Arriving on time and in good condition, we enjoyed a very pleasant evening. The food and conversation were both top notch, and Papa and Eva, it seemed to me, were on their best behavior.

The first hint of a problem didn't come until we were leaving.

Eva, who had slipped her shoes off before dinner, discovered that she couldn't get them on again. She ended up carrying them to the car.

"Shall I drive, Eva?" I asked hopefully. I had made similar offers on myriad occasions, and the answer had never been yes.

"I'm perfectly fine to drive," Eva said, climbing into the car. "I'll just drive barefoot!"

"I don't think it's legal to drive barefoot," I commented, pulling the passenger seat back so that Papa could climb into the back of their sedan.

"Maybe not," Papa said, "but it's a damn fool law if you can't drive without shoes on! What the hell difference would it make?"

"I do it all the time in the summer," Eva said. "The heat makes my feet swell!"

Papa, who was willing to argue from a variety of viewpoints, suggested, "You need a larger size of shoe, darling."

"I do not, Pat! You know I've always worn a size four!"

"You've always worn a size four," Papa said. "And you can't get them on your feet because they don't fit properly, darling!" He settled into the back seat as Eva checked the car mirrors.

"You don't know anything about it, Pat!" she said.

"I don't know anything about it," Papa echoed. "Of course, you still can't get your shoes on, darling, and my shoes always fit me."

"Oh, just be quiet!" Eva said.

I decided it would be a bad time to reintroduce the seatbelt argument, and we set off unbuckled for the ten minute ride home. Papa quieted down for a brief nap in the back, while Eva began happily to discuss the wonderful evening we'd had with their friends. As she made a right turn, I mentally noted the multi-lane road a short distance ahead, and particularly the red light in our direction.

She just has a habit of driving faster than I do, I told myself. She sees it. Don't be so nervous.

She must see it.

Doesn't she see it?

She doesn't see it!

"Eva," I said sharply, "you've got a red light there."

"I know!" Eva sounded irritated, but she immediately hit the brake hard.

The brakes shrieked, slowing us, not stopping us, as I noticed in the traffic on the cross road a gasoline tanker, looking to be in the perfect position for a collision with us, and he had a green light. I thrust out a hand to the dashboard to keep myself in place as our car slid into a traffic lane. With a tremendous double-bang sound, we were hit by the truck.

When we came to a stop, Eva was crying and flustered. My wrist hurt, but I could move it. Papa, startled out of his nap in the back seat, said, "What in the hell happened?"

"We were in an accident, Papa," I said. "We have to get out of the car!" I was very afraid of the possibility of a fire, and opened the door and pulled my seat forward to let Papa out of the back.

"An accident," Papa muttered as he climbed out of the car.

"Come on, Eva, we have to get out!" I said.

"I don't even know how that happened!" she said. "He was driving much too fast!"

The truck driver peered in at Eva through her window. "Are you all right?" he asked. "Is everyone all right?"

Eva continued crying.

"I think we're just shaken up," I said.

"Thank God!" he said. "I had the green, and she came right into my lane out of nowhere! I hit my brakes and I swerved, but I didn't have room to go into the next lane and I couldn't stop in time to avoid her! Thank God my tank was almost empty!"

Within minutes, people were directing traffic around us, and police arrived on the scene. Eva, meanwhile, continued to sit in the car.

"Eva," I said, "get out of the car. We can't drive it home like this."

"My car door won't open!" she said.

"Then climb out this side," I encouraged her. She finally slid over onto the passenger side, and was about to step out onto the pavement in her bare feet. "There's a lot of broken glass on the street, Eva," I told her. "You have to put on your shoes!"

"I can't!" she said.

"You have to!" I insisted. "Otherwise you'll cut your feet!"

"Oh, darn!" She fumbled for her shoes, and then tried to wedge her toes into them. As she stood, she suddenly cried out in pain. "Oh!"

"Are you all right?" I asked.

"Are you injured, darling?" Papa said.

"These shoes hurt my feet, Pat!" she said, making a small cry with each step.

"The G-D shoes!" Papa said. "Here, darling, hold my arm! There, there!"

A policeman hurried over to me. "Shall I call an ambulance for her?"

"No, she's O.K." I felt very silly as I told him, "It's just that her feet are swollen from the heat, so her shoes hurt her."

The accident had happened right by a gas station with a phone booth outside. Handing me some coins, Papa instructed me to call Norm and Paul, and ask them to pick us up and bring us back to the apartment.

Still shuffling painfully in her tiny shoes, Eva looked up. "And make sure you don't worry them!" she added.

I wondered how to word "We were hit by a gasoline truck" in a reassuring way.

Happily, by the next morning at breakfast, we were all doing fine except for a few minor aches and pains. "Our insurance company will call you for an account of what happened," Papa told me.

"You can explain to them that it wasn't my fault," Eva said.

"I think the car's a total loss," Papa said, "but the important thing is no one was hurt."

"You're right, Pat! No one was hurt," Eva said. "See, Kay? You don't need seatbelts at all!"

# 32

## So Difficult

On one of my weekend visits, when Papa went off to the race track for the day. Eva and I had spent some of the morning looking over drawings I had done in an art class I was taking. Eva loved art, other than the modern variety, and she enjoyed looking at my drawings. She particularly liked one sketch I had made of a rag doll.

"Isn't it darling!" she said.

"I can do a sketch of the doll for you," I told her.

"I would love it," she said. "Well, you know I love dolls."

"I know," I said, and indeed I did. In the guest room where I slept, the bed was covered with a large collection of stuffed animals, clown dolls and other cloth dolls which I had to clear away before I could get to sleep.

"When you make my drawing," she said, "I'll hang it on this wall, right next to this charcoal landscape you did when you were a little girl." The wall outside the guest room was covered with a variety of framed items, paintings, drawings, prints, photos, even a huge leaf Eva had scooped up when it fell to the ground during a visit she made to Winterthur. Part of the display was a framed drawing of a snowy house and yard I had done when I was eight, a project from a Jon Nagy drawing set. Right next to my rendition was my mother's framed drawing of the same scene.

"It's so nice that you kept that drawing," I said.

"Well, of course I did," she said. "You and your mother are so talented! I never could draw."

In the early afternoon, we sat down to a bountiful lunch, just the two of us.

"You know, I'm so glad to see how you've matured," Eva said. "You were a very cold person as a child."

"Me?" I was mystified.

"You were very difficult to talk to," she answered.

"I was not," I said.

"You were!"

"What do you mean, Eva?"

"I never could get a conversation going with you."

"I was a little shy," I admitted.

"It was more than that. I'd ask you things, and you just wouldn't answer me," Eva continued.

"I wouldn't answer you when you asked something? I don't remember ever doing that."

"Oh, you'd answer," Eva said. "You just wouldn't tell me anything."

"Hmmm," I said. Oh, oh. This was becoming clearer. There had been times when I wouldn't talk freely. Like the time she asked me which brother I didn't get along with. Or the time she scolded me for not crying when I cut my knee.

"It was so frustrating! I was trying to get to know you better, and you always closed me out! I felt so excluded."

It occurred to me that I had been raised to dislike Eva, not to give her a chance. My mother and my maternal grandmother were very critical of Eva, blaming her for Papa leaving his wife and children, even though that marriage was failing before Eva was ever on the scene. It must have been hard for her when I was a child and she and Papa visited my family, because we had all seen her as an outsider. "I'm sorry, Eva," I said.

Well, you don't do that anymore. I'm so glad we can talk now."

"I'm glad too, Eva."

"But you were so difficult as a child!"

# 33

# Stories Papa Told Me

Papa was a storyteller, and over the years, he shared many, many tales of his life, some of which I heard several times, but some, only once. These are some of those stories as he told them to me.

*I hate fish; always have. I've told you that when I was a child, we'd have fish for dinner at least once a week. It was what we had, and I was to eat it, but I couldn't get it past my lips. My father would insist, and I'd refuse. Finally, he'd send me up to bed without any supper. My mother would watch sadly as I left the room. But after dinner, when her cleaning was done, she'd always sneak food to me up the back stairs.*

*Fool that I was, when I had children of my own, I insisted they eat fish. Couldn't stand it either, and yet I said they had to eat it. I thought it would be good for them, that they would learn to like it. Your mother couldn't stomach it any more than I could, and I'd make her sit at the table until she ate her fish.*

*   *      *      *

*My brother Alfredo was the oldest child. When our mother emigrated, he stayed in Italy, never came to the United States. He joined the military. He and I corresponded for a long time, but we never met face to face.*

*My brother Guido was the next oldest. When Mamma came to this country, Guido was left behind with Uncle the Priest. Ha! She wanted Guido to become a priest! But as he grew up, he was too interested in the girls. Uncle the Priest wrote my mother and told her that it wasn't going to work, Guido wasn't cut out for the priesthood, and so Guido too came to this country, but he came as a young man.*

*My brother Tav – his name was Ottavio, but we called him Tav – he was born in Italy too. He was much bigger and older than I; when I was a boy, he seemed like a man. He was often sick. I remember him closed up in a room, coughing and coughing, horrible coughing. I imagine now that he had tuberculosis, though no one said that at the time. But he survived.*

*My brother Gene – we called him Gino in the family, but he decided to become Gene – he was older than I. He and I never got along. He was just like our father.*

92

*Algesa was the youngest, and the only girl. She was three, almost four, years younger than I.*

* * * *

*My parents loved opera. We had a Victrola, and they played 78s of the great masters. They wanted us to know opera. They wanted us to get an education. In Italy, if you had no money, there were two ways to get an education. You could go into the military, or you could go into the priesthood. Alfredo went into the military. My mother tried to get Guido into the priesthood, although it didn't take. But here, in America, everyone could get an education.*

* * * *

*I've never known why I was named Armando. I can't remember my parents ever mentioning an Armando, and there were no family friends of that name. My mother gave me the middle name of Raphael after her brother, Uncle the Priest. I Americanized it to Ralph, but my mother had me baptized Armando Raphael.*

* * * *

*After my mother died, we had a year of mourning. When the year of mourning had ended, we took off our black arm bands, and my father went back to Italy to find another wife. He married a woman named Emma and brought her back. She was a kind woman; she was good to me. But after a time, my father decided that he wanted to move back to Italy, and he expected that my sister and I would go with him. I was in high school then. I told him I wouldn't go. Italy was his country, not mine. I was an American. He tried to convince me that it would be good for me, but I wouldn't do it. He finally arranged for me to stay here with my brother Guido and his wife Aurelia. I stayed with them, and Guido took over Kelly's Hats.*

*My sister went with my father to Italy. I didn't know how she could do it, because she was an American too, like me. I was so angry with her for going, but she went with him anyway, and I never saw her again.*

*My father came back to this country to visit. It was after I had graduated from high school. I worked for a time as a reporter for a paper in Boston, but I had decided to go to college. My father asked me again to come to Italy. I said, no, I was going to start college at the University of New Hampshire.*

*"In Italy," he said, "we have great universities, much better than American colleges. You can get a better education in Italy!" But I wouldn't go. I'm an American, and I wanted an American education.*

*Some years later, after my father had died, after I was married and had a family, my brother Guido wrote me and told me that our sister Algesa wanted to marry, there was a young man who wanted to marry her, but that she didn't have enough money for the dowry. Guido, as the oldest family member in this country, was asking all his younger brothers to contribute money for Algesa's dowry.*

*I wouldn't do it. I wouldn't give a cent. It was during the Depression, and money was tight, but that wasn't why. I told Guido that Algesa is an American, and Americans don't do it that way. Americans don't pay people to marry them. If her young man loved Algesa, he would marry her without the money, and if he wouldn't marry her without money, she was better off without him. But I would not give one cent for my sister to buy a husband.*

*The other brothers contributed. Maybe they didn't come up with enough, I don't know, but she never married. She lives with one of Alfredo's sons and his family in Rome now. We send cards. We talk occasionally on the phone, and we're cordial, but I don't know her anymore.*

# 34

# The Perfect Gift for Papa

As far back as I could remember, every year, my mother would shop desperately for a birthday gift for Papa. "He wants a shirt," she'd say, her brow furrowed with worry. "It has to have two pockets. Last year I bought him a shirt with only one breast pocket, and he said he couldn't wear it. He needs two pockets." She'd scour the department stores and, most especially, the very expensive men's clothing stores, in her search for the perfect shirt for Papa. Finally, she would find an unreasonably priced shirt with reasonable fabric, perhaps a subtle print, and sporting two breast pockets. Success!

Or so it seemed, until Papa received the gift. "Hmmmm," he'd say.

"What's wrong, Papa?" she'd ask.

"Nothing, nothing," he'd answer, "only the pockets are small. I don't wear pockets for decoration! I need room to put things in them. There's not any room to put my pencils and notes in these pockets!"

Should my mother be lucky enough to find a shirt with the right sized pockets, you can be sure that Papa would find the sleeves were too long, too wide, too narrow, with the wrong kind of cuff, or perhaps the problem was with the collar.

Some years, she'd try to please him with books, which on the surface seemed a safe choice. Papa loved to read. She'd look for titles that had been favorably reviewed and that dealt with a favorite subject of his: the American Revolution, Thomas Jefferson, horse racing, Abraham Lincoln, politics.

"Hmmmm," Papa would say. "Nothing new in it." Or, rolling his eyes, and with a sneer in his voice, "Hmmmm. This fellow worked for *Eisenhower*!" Or, "I'm not sure who he was really writing about, but it certainly wasn't Jefferson." Or, "I wonder if this fellow has *ever* had an original thought."

My mother despaired of finding a gift that would please her father, and as an adult, I had my own struggle to find a satisfactory gift for Papa.

One of my efforts was inspired by Papa's story of his childhood of oatmeal breakfasts. I took up the search for rough textured oatmeal for Papa. On one visit, I brought him McCann's Steel Cut Irish Oatmeal. Papa looked skeptical. "We can try it out for breakfast tomorrow," he said.

"But, Pat," Eva said, "I made bread to have for toast with bacon and eggs this weekend!"

"Then I'll try the oatmeal Monday," he said. "Still, I have my doubts."

When I next called, Papa informed me, "That oatmeal you brought – it was good for what it was, but it wasn't at all like the oatmeal my mother used. Best thing in the world! Never since had anything like it! You just can't get it anymore."

I gave up on oatmeal, but the next thing I tried was cookies, also because of one of Papa's stories: "We had a bakery just across the street from us when I was a boy," he said. "Sometimes my mother would buy day-old cookies there. It was the cheapest kind of cookie they sold – just a plain sugar cookie. Sometimes what she bought was just a bag of broken pieces. But she'd put those broken pieces into our bowls, and pour our hot cocoa over them. My sister and I would eat them with spoons for our breakfast as a treat. They were cheap and plain, but I've never had a better cookie in my life. You just can't find cookies like that anymore!"

I consulted a variety of cook books, settled on a recipe and brought homemade cookies when I returned for a visit. Eva was excited. "What kind?" she asked.

"Butter cookies," I answered.

She eagerly opened the tin. "There's no icing," she announced, her disappointment clear.

"I was trying to make a plain cookie, like the ones Papa's mother bought at the bakery," I said.

"I don't like plain things," Eva said.

Papa grabbed the tin from Eva's hands, pulled out a cookie and took a bite. "Hmmm." He rendered his verdict: "It's a good cookie, but it's not at all like those cookies my mother got us. These taste of butter. They're rich. My mother bought cheap cookies, the cheapest cookies they made. But they were delicious! Best cookies I ever ate!"

Papa ate my disappointing cookies nonetheless.

On other visits, I brought other cookie experiments I'd tried – butter cookies, sugar cookies, dropped, rolled, or otherwise shaped, some plain, with a few adorned with icing or sprinkles for Eva – but no luck. I should have realized that nothing could ever match Papa's early memories of those cookies, but I was a slow learner in that regard.

I was intrigued when I read a review on **Ethnic at Large**, a memoir by Jerre Mangione, who had also grown up the American born son of Italian immigrants. Although Mangione was a younger man, I thought Papa would find in the book parallels to his own life. I read a good bit of it, and I began to think I had found the perfect birthday gift for Papa.

When I presented it to him, Papa carefully unfolded the wrapping paper.

"What is it, Pat?" Eva asked.

"Hmmmm," he said, turning the book over, studying the jacket, before opening it and paging through. "Interesting. Thank you, thank you." He pulled my face closer for a kiss, and I was glad he liked my choice of book.

When we retired late that evening, Papa took up his new book and announced that he wasn't tired yet and was going to read. It turned out that he stayed up almost all night reading his new book.

The next morning at breakfast, he said, "Well, I finished that book you gave me."

"What did you think?" I asked.

"It had its points," Papa allowed. "But there was too much talk about sex."

"About sex?" I asked, wondering if we were talking about the same book.

"It's the fashion these days," Papa said. "No matter what the book is about, people can't write a book without talking about sex. And, really, if you think about it, there is nothing – "

"Don't start, Pat," Eva warned.

"There is nothing, absolutely nothing, as ridiculous as the act of two people having intercourse. Nothing whatsoever!"

"Oh, stop that, Pat! There is nothing wrong with sex!"

"I didn't say that there is anything wrong with it," Papa said. "We're drawn by it. We enjoy it. We long for it. And some damn fools want to write about it. But, still, there is nothing in the world that looks so ridiculous as two people engaged in the sexual act! Think about it! The positions we take!"

"How can you say that?" Eva demanded. "What's ridiculous about it?"

"What's ridiculous about it?" he roared.

As they dug in with their argument, I realized that it might be better to leave Papa's boyhood memories out of it when I tried to find a gift that he might actually like.

While out shopping with a friend one time, I unexpectedly came across an item that had Papa written all over it – a mug, the perfect size for his coffee, and it was emblazoned with the sentence, "There are two sides to every argument – mine, and the wrong one." I bought it, and a pretty cup and saucer for Eva too. This time I was certain: I had found the perfect gifts!

So, on my next trip to Maryland, I surprised them with small wrapped packages. Eva crowed with delight at her cup and saucer, sniffling with joy, but she was always pleased with the gifts I gave her. Papa pulled his mug from its box and read it aloud, a hint of a smile playing at his lips. "It's almost perfect," he said, getting up from the table. "I need a marker so I can fix it." He rummaged through a kitchen drawer, and came up with a fine point permanent marker, carrying it back to the kitchen table, where he sat and edited his mug.

"What are you doing, Pat?" Eva asked.

"You'll see. You'll see," he said.

Finally, he waved it in front of her face, while reciting to her the amended mug message: "There are two sides to every issue – mine, and the wrong one – Eva's!"

Apparently, it hadn't been perfect, but, at last, I had found an *almost* perfect gift for Papa.

After Papa's birthday, my mother mentioned to me that he had again found fault with a gift she gave him. "He wanted a sweater. He said it should be a cardigan, and he wanted side pockets in it. I looked and looked and looked, and finally found one for him in his size. It had everything he asked for, but now he says the sleeves are too long!"

"Of course the sleeves are too long," I said. "They don't make men's sweaters to fit men who are five feet tall."

"I think he hates it," she said. "He has to roll up the sleeves."

"He rolls up the sleeves on all his sweaters," I said.

"He never likes the gifts I give him! They're never right."

"Mum, I don't think there's such a thing as a gift that's right for Papa. He likes getting gifts, but he likes complaining about them even more than he likes the gift itself."

"Maybe," she said.

I told her about the book I had given him. "Don't feel hurt," I said. "Nothing is ever exactly right for Papa."

I was wrong, though.

Accustomed to their evening and Sunday morning rituals of watching and arguing through the newscasts and political discussion on television, I discovered to my surprise that Papa and Eva were regular viewers of another program unrelated to politics. Not only were they fans of "The Muppet Show;" they didn't even argue about it.

"Don't you just love Kermit!" Eva exclaimed. "He's so bashful!"

"Miss Piggy's batting her eyelashes again," Papa pointed out. "He doesn't stand a chance against *her*."

"Aren't they darling!" Eva said. "They're so funny!"

"And wait till you see those two fellows who sit in the audience and complain!" Papa added. "I love the two of them!"

"Don't forget that darling dog!" Eva said. "We love all the Muppets!"

On a subsequent shopping excursion, I found something that I thought might bring them a chuckle. Next visit, I presented them with the gift.

"Oh, look, Pat!" Eva began to cry as she opened the small box.

Papa beamed. "Will you look at that! It's a soap in the shape of Kermit the Frog!"

"Green soap," Eva said, sniffling. "Oh, look at the little paddle Kermit's holding!"

"Don't cry, darling."

"I can't help it, Pat!"

"Look at his mouth, darling. He looks like he's singing!"

"Oh, I just love it so!" Eva exclaimed.

"It's perfect," Papa said. "Perfect!"

Kermit took up permanent residence, and no one ever washed with him. On all my visits thereafter, When I stepped into their bathroom, I'd see on top of the sink, nestled in a dish, Kermit the Soap.

For once in my life, I had found a perfect gift for Papa.

# 35

# Brunch with Papa and Eva

One morning when Papa was at the racetrack, and I was spending the day with Eva, she asked me, "Do you like brunches?"

"I love brunches!" I answered.

"Good!" she said. "Your Poppa can be a little cheap sometimes, you know. Remember when he used to send five dollar checks for you and your brothers at Christmas time?"

"Yes."

"Well, I told him that just wasn't right! I told him, 'Pat, they're your grandchildren! You should give them each ten dollars!' And I kept arguing with him about it every year until finally he gave in and raised it to seven-fifty, but that's as high as he'd go!"

"Oh," I said. I remembered those checks.

"It's not that we don't have the money," Eva said. "We have plenty of money, but he always wants to save it. He doesn't want to spend it on gifts, and he doesn't see why we should go out to eat when we can have breakfast at home. But Woody's has a wonderful brunch! Your Poppa loves it too, even though he won't admit it. It's a buffet, and you can have as much as you want! They have all kinds of things, the plain things like eggs and bacon and pancakes, and all kinds of pastries too! They have everything you can think of to eat at a brunch! We haven't been there for ages, and he won't argue about the cost in front of you, so I'll just tell your Poppa we have to take you out for brunch, and we'll go to Woody's tomorrow morning!"

The next morning found us seated at Woody's, Eva and I on one side of the table, Papa on the other, all of us with heaped plates in front of us. Papa seemed as pleased as Eva and I were. "I love bacon and eggs," he said. "Eva used to make them for me every day for breakfast. And then the doctor told me I have arteriosclerosis. No more than two eggs a week, that's what he told me."

"I stopped cooking the eggs," Eva commented.

"She didn't stop cooking the eggs!" Papa said. "She couldn't make them for me, but she cooked them for the dog!"

"Well, we still had Noey when you were first diagnosed, Pat. Noey was used to eating bacon and eggs, and *he* didn't have a cholesterol problem."

"I know we still had the damn dog. I used to sit and watch Noey eat his bacon and eggs, while all I had was my miserable little bowl of cereal."

"How can you call Noey a damn dog, Pat? You know you loved him!"

"I didn't love him when he was eating my eggs at breakfast!"

Eva giggled. "Your Poppa used to get so mad!"

"She'd cook liver for that dog too," Papa added. "I love liver! I'd sit there drooling while the dog ate it, but no liver for me because I had to watch my cholesterol!"

"Well, you can indulge yourself today, Pat," Eva said.

"That's what I'm doing!" He shifted some egg and bacon onto a crust of toast and popped it into his mouth.

I was enjoying a light, flaky biscuit along with my scrambled eggs. "How's the biscuit?" Eva asked.

"It's very good," I said.

"Break off a piece for her," Papa suggested.

"No, don't bother," Eva said. "You know I don't like plain things, Pat."

"You should try this cherry pastry, darling," Papa offered. "It has nuts."

She took a bite of his pastry. "Maybe I'll get one when I go back up to the buffet, but I'll see if I can find one with more icing. What's in that coffee cake you have?" Eva asked me.

"Blueberries," I said. "Want to try it?"

"Just a little corner." She stabbed at it with her fork and took a nibble. "Mmmm! It's buttery!"

A little later, we all returned to survey the buffet a second time. When Eva came back to the table, she was ecstatic. "Look what I found!" she said. In one hand, she held a plate stacked high with an assortment of pastries, muffins and coffee cakes as well as three biscuits, and, in the other hand, she carried a stack of napkins. "They have an apricot cake with almonds!"

"Apricots!" Papa said approvingly, spearing a slice of coffee cake from her plate.

"Don't take the whole thing, Pat! Leave some for me!"

Papa broke off a piece to taste and returned the rest to Eva. "Not too sweet," he said.

"Not too sweet?" Eva asked. "Oh, darn! Then you keep it, Pat!"

"All the more for me," he said.

"And I got some more biscuits for you," Eva told me. "You said you liked them."

"I can't eat all those biscuits!" I protested.

"Not for now," Eva explained. "You can have them later." She began wrapping the biscuits in some of her napkins.

"Eva, you're not allowed to take food home from a buffet!" I said.

"You're just being silly," she said.

"There was a sign, right by the door when we came in!"

"Nonsense," Papa commented. "People take things from the buffet all the time. The restaurant expects it."

Eva had finished wrapping biscuits, and was moving on to the muffins. "Your Poppa always takes home some artificial sweetener when we go to a restaurant. Everyone does!"

Papa stuck a hand in his sweater pocket and pulled out a packet to show me.

Meanwhile, Eva's pile of napkin-wrapped sweets was growing. "Look at that family leaving now," she said. "The little girl is taking an apple."

"It's just one little kid with one little apple," I said.

"I told you! Everyone does it! But don't worry! No one will even see!" She reached for the large shoulder bag which was hanging on the back of my chair, then lifted its flap and began to drop her stash into *my* purse.

Later, as we waited for Papa to pay the bill, I adjusted the position of my purse strap on my shoulder. Eva leaned toward me and said, "I hate carrying a purse! But I'm so glad you carry a big one!" I had certainly noticed she didn't bring one herself. I wondered what I'd say if the manager confronted me about all that food she had crammed into my shoulder bag.

My grandparents made me do it?

Several months later, when I called to tell Eva I could again come for a weekend, she was delighted. "You know," she said, "Pat and I haven't been back to Woody's since that time we went with you. I'll tell your Poppa that you loved it last time, and we'll have to take you back for brunch this Sunday!"

Forewarned is forearmed, so when I went to Maryland that weekend, I was carrying the tiniest purse I owned. I could barely squeeze my wallet and a comb into it; there was no way that Eva would be able to stash any of her loot with me!

On Sunday morning as we prepared to leave the house to go for brunch, I felt it was only fair to warn Eva. "Oh, Eva," I said, "I just realized all I brought with me was this tiny little purse! You won't be able to fit anything from the restaurant into it."

"Oh, darn!" Eva said. "Now I'll have to bring a purse myself!" I followed her into her bedroom, where she began rummaging through her walk-in closet. "I wonder which purse I should bring!"

I was only joking, but I still can't understand what possessed me to resort to sarcasm. "Why don't you bring a tote bag?"

"What a good idea!" Eva said. She retreated further into the closet and emerged with a large, completely empty tote bag, into which she dropped a tube of lipstick. Then the three of us set off for Woody's.

Again, the food was great, but this time, I found it even harder to relax. As we ate, Eva kept asking Papa and me, "Do you like that?" If either of us said, "It's good!" or "Want to try some?" or even a simple, "Yes," Eva would return to the buffet to get some more of the favored item for us to take home with us. My anxiety rose with every napkin-wrapped item Eva dropped into her tote bag, and I stopped admitting to her that I liked anything.

"Look, darling!" Papa said, returning from one trip back to the buffet. "They've just put out some barbecued ribs!"

"We love ribs!" Eva told me. She hurried up to the buffet and came back with a full-sized dinner plate completely covered with ribs stacked two inches high. If we had invited the party at the next table to join us, we still wouldn't have been able to eat all those ribs! Eva did eat one or two of them. But what to do about the rest of them, all shiny and sticky with barbecue sauce?

She flagged down a manager. "Excuse me," she said, "but I just can't finish all of my ribs. Would you please get me some foil, and I'll take them home so they won't go to waste!" I can't say he looked happy about it, but the manager brought her several long sheets of foil, and Eva's carefully wrapped ribs also disappeared into her tote bag.

By the time we finished eating, the tote bag was bulging with goodies. As Eva and I stood beyond the register, waiting for Papa to settle the bill, she gleefully pushed the bag toward me. "Feel how heavy my tote bag is!" she said.

"No, thank you," I answered, staring at the ceiling in the opposite corner of the room from where Eva stood.

"Well, it's very heavy!" she said.

"I'm sure it is." I continued to study the ceiling.

"You won't even look at me, will you?" Eva demanded.

"Not until we're safely in the car," I answered.

"I think you're trying to pretend you're not with me!"

"I am."

"Are you always like this?" she asked.

I stared at the ceiling, imagining scenes of the manager detaining us, or perhaps the police waiting for us in the parking lot. "Believe it or not, Eva, I've never been in this situation before."

"Hmmmph!" said Eva. "You're behaving so strangely!"

But no one stopped us from getting into the car and driving away. We made it home without incident. Eva spent the next hour rearranging her refrigerator, which as usual was already totally full to start with. But she was a miracle worker when it came to packaging food, and, as always, she managed to find a place for everything.

A few months later, Eva sadly informed me, "I'm so disappointed! Woody's has discontinued their brunch!"

"It's just as well," Papa said. "You make wonderful breakfasts here at home. And no one can ever eat enough at a restaurant to justify their prices."

# 36

# Papa and the Racetrack

"You know how it was that I became interested in horse racing?" Papa asked.

"No, Papa."

"Hmmmph. It was back when your mother was a child and I was teaching English at Canisius College. We used to come east and stay the summer in Malden with your grandmother's family. Spent a lot of time with your grandmother's twin Helena and her husband Bump."

"I remember Uncle Bumpy," I said. "He used to come to our house for our birthdays when I was little."

"Oh, Bump was quite a fellow. Worked for the railroad. We were very different, had very different interests, but I always enjoyed him. One day he said to me, 'Pat, I'm going to the track. Why don't you come along?'

"There I was, a dapper little guy with a dapper little mustache, a college man, young professor, intellectual, nose always in a book! 'Fine,' I said, and off we went. We got to the track, and I entered a different world! The horses and the jockeys, the stands full of people, the sights and the sounds, the colors and the crowds! Bump introduced me to his friends, told them I was married to his wife's sister, taught in a college. Ha! Taught in a college!

"We went to the window to place our bets. I didn't know a damn thing about horses in those days, had never been to a race track before, had no idea whatsoever how to choose a horse! Well, they all began to tell me about it. 'You don't want that one, Professor! He'll be dead last!' They called me 'Professor.'

"I had the time of my life! Loved it! Kept going back to the track with Bump all that summer. Still going." He looked down into his mug. "Any more coffee?" he asked.

I poured more coffee for both of us.

Papa swirled the coffee in his mug, sipped. "People have interests, pastimes, hobbies. They go to football games, they golf, they collect stamps. It costs them money, but they budget to spend some of their money on things that bring them pleasure. For me, it's horses. That's what I enjoy.

I budget how much money I'm going to spend each year on entertaining myself at the track. I budget how much money I'll wager. And I stick to that budget. And if I lost all of what I bet – every cent of it – it wouldn't matter financially because it's what I planned to spend on my entertainment. But I don't lose it all. I keep records. I make a small amount of money every year from betting on horses. I don't win every time I go to the track. Sometimes I lose. I may lose money on several different days. But I beat chance. Taking the year as a whole, I beat chance.

"How? I study. I learn everything I can about the horses, the jockeys, the owners, the training, the race tracks. I work at it. I analyze it. And so I beat chance every year. The year I can't beat chance will be the year I stop betting on horses."

"I'd love to go to the track with you sometime, Papa," I said.

"No." He shook his head. "I wouldn't take you. You'd hate it. Loud. Full of smoke."

"I wouldn't mind."

"No, not the right kind of place for you at all. I wouldn't take you."

I thought in time I might be able to talk Papa into bringing me with him to the racetrack, but I was wrong. The Professor just couldn't see it as a place to bring his granddaughter, who, like him, always had her nose in a book.

# 37

## The Reagan Years

We sat at the kitchen table over dinner, watching the evening news. "Goddamn it!" Papa shouted. "Look at him! Just look at him!"

"We know, Pat," Eva said. "We already know!"

"He's a goddamned actor!" Papa continued. "He's just reading his lines. He doesn't know a damn thing about the government. And all the damn fools watch him and think he's such a good President! They don't realize that he's still playing a part in a B movie!"

"We can't stand Reagan," Eva told me.

"He's a charlatan!" Papa said. "An empty-headed fool!"

"Your Poppa called the White House to complain," Eva said.

"I called the White House every day! And you know what they did?" Papa asked. "The White House operator asked my name! She wanted to take it down!"

"It made him so mad!" Eva added.

"I told her, I am an American citizen, that's who I am, and that's enough! But she always wants to write down my name, and she wants to know where I'm from. She wants my goddamned address! Well, I'm not going to give it to her!"

"He's given her quite an argument!" Eva explained.

"Of course I give her an argument!" Papa said. "What are we coming to, that the White House is making a list of the names of people who complain! Are we blacklisting people again? Back to that bastard McCarthy? But she won't budge an inch. She has to take the names, she says. She's instructed to take the names! I've called the White House for years, I told her, and I've never given my name! But, no, no, that's the policy now, she said. She has to take my name! Just obeying orders! So that's it! I've given up calling them altogether!"

"Tell her what you've been doing instead, Pat," Eva instructed, giving a little giggle.

"Well," Papa said, "I go out on my little errands. I've taken up stopping at the supermarket every day. I check out what they have to offer in the meat department, and I position myself right beside the most expensive cut of meat I find."

"Yes?" I prompted.

"And then I wait. Sooner or later, someone comes along. 'Look at that tenderloin, lady,' I say to her. 'Isn't that a beautiful cut of meat?'

"'Why, yes,' she'll say.

"'Wouldn't that make a wonderful dinner for your family tonight?' I ask. 'Why don't you buy it for them?'

"'Oh, no,' she'll say. 'I can't buy that!'

"'Why not?' I ask. 'You said it's beautiful! Why won't you buy it for them?'

"'I can't,' she says, 'It's too expensive!'

"'Too expensive?' I say. 'Well, let me ask you one question. Who did you vote for in the last election?'

"'What?' she says. 'What?'

"I make it simple for her. 'Who did you vote for in the last Presidential election?' I ask. 'Did you vote for Reagan?'

"'Why, yes, I did,' she says.

"Now I've got her where I want her. 'Hell, then,' I say, 'you deserve these prices!' And I stomp off."

A few months later during another of my visits, Eva, chuckling, informed me, "Your Poppa had another problem with Reagan. Tell her, Pat!"

"Oh, that!" Papa said, shaking his head. "It's Eva's fault! She loves ballet!"

"Well, you know I studied ballet as a girl," Eva said. "Of course I love ballet! But your Poppa and I have a subscription series to a lot of cultural events in the district."

"But this one was ballet!" Papa reminded.

"Of course, when we go to a performance, we make a big night of it, and we go out to eat before the show," Eva said. "Always to the same place."

"There's a restaurant at the Kennedy Center," Papa said. "So we eat dinner there. Very convenient."

"And the food is wonderful," Eva said. "But what your Poppa really likes there – oh, show her, Pat!"

Papa went to the silverware drawer and retrieved a teaspoon. "Here it is," he said, waving a spoon at me. "This is what caused the whole damn problem."

"Your Poppa just loves the spoons they have at the restaurant!" Eva said.

"Just the perfect size and shape," Papa told me. "Fits easily in the hand."

"It is a nice spoon," I agreed.

"So when we went to that restaurant – " Eva began

"We don't go often," Papa said.

"Your Poppa stole a spoon."

"I'd love to have a full set," Papa said.

"I think one is enough!" Eva said.

"Maybe so, maybe so." He folded his arms across his chest.

"Well, we were going to a ballet recently," she continued.

"Joffrey," Papa interrupted.

"A traveling company," Eva explained. "And we went out to dinner first, and your Poppa picked up a spoon."

"I stuck it in my jacket pocket while we were eating dessert," Papa said. "They didn't notice a thing."

"And so we left the restaurant, but when we arrived for the ballet, there was a huge line."

"Young Reagan dances with the Joffrey now," Papa said. "He was one of the performers."

"We knew that in advance," Eva said.

"But what we didn't know," Papa said, "was that President and Mrs. Reagan were going to be attending the performance the night we went. And of course they had all kinds of security there,

Secret Service all over the place. But the reason for all the lines, what was really holding everything up, was that everyone going into the theater had to go through a metal detector first. And here I am with the spoon in my pocket. As soon as I tried to pass through the detector, I set off all kinds of alarms. Buzzing! Bells! Oh, lord!" He laughed and ran his hand through his hair.

"They pulled your Poppa out of line," Eva said.

"And I had to account for myself," Papa said. "They interrogated me. They wanted to know why I was trying to get into that theater with a teaspoon, a damn teaspoon!"

"I told them we had just gone out to eat," Eva said, "and I fibbed a little. I said that your Poppa must have picked it up accidentally from the restaurant, so it was all a mistake."

"So they let me go," Papa said. He laughed again. "But what the hell kind of damage did they think I was going to do with one little stainless steel teaspoon?"

# 38

# A Gentleman Caller

I phoned Papa and Eva to arrange to visit one weekend. "A friend is driving through Maryland on the way to visit his family and he offered to give me a ride," I told them.

"A man?" Eva asked. "What's his name?"

"Mitch" I answered.

"And when will we meet him?"

"He's just a friend," I said. "We're not dating."

"Maybe that will change," Eva suggested. "You never know."

"Anyway," I said, "if you can give me directions from the highway to the apartment – "

Papa, who was on the extension, interrupted. "It's too complicated," he said. "Your friend will never be able to find us! But there's a convenience store just off the highway. I'll tell you how to get there from the Baltimore Washington Expressway. Then, when you get to the convenience store, call me and I'll come pick you up right away."

"But, Papa, if you give me directions," I began.

"No, it'd be much too difficult for him," he said, and that was that.

On the Friday evening following that conversation, I called as instructed from the convenience store and then waited about ten minutes in Mitch's car for Papa to arrive. Finally, Papa pulled into the lot, parked, and climbed out of his car. He was wearing an old jacket, a wool cap, and had his hands shoved into his pants pockets.

I opened the car door and waved. "Hi, Papa," I called.

"There you are!" He came quickly to my side and gave me a sloppy wet kiss. Meanwhile, Mitch got my suitcase out of the trunk. Without a word to Mitch, Papa grabbed the suitcase. "Anything else to carry?" he asked me.

"No, Papa," I said, "That's all, but –"

"Then we'd better get going! Eva's got dinner ready," Papa said. He hadn't even acknowledged Mitch's existence.

"But, Papa, I'd like you to meet my friend Mitch!"

Papa turned and glanced at the fellow. "Hello, Mitch," he muttered. "There, I've met him," he told me. "Are you satisfied now?"

"It's nice to meet you, sir," Mitch said to Papa's back, as Papa stalked away to his own car with my suitcase.

When we got to the apartment, Eva greeted me smiling, wooden spoon in hand. "Your friend didn't follow you over?" she asked.

"No," I said. "He has a good drive still ahead of him."

"Well, what was he like, Pat?" she asked, turning to Papa. But before Papa could respond, Eva gasped. "Just look at you, Pat! Why did you wear those ratty old pants? And the jacket with the hole in it, Pat!" She turned to me. "I keep telling him he has to get rid of that jacket, but he just won't do it!"

"Hmphh!" Papa said.

"How could you, Pat! Dressing like that and embarrassing your granddaughter in front of her friend!"

Papa's voice rose to the occasion. "I don't see why I have to get dressed up to meet some young fool!"

"Pat!" Eva positively shrieked.

"What?" he grunted.

"You're not wearing your teeth! You went to meet the young man and you weren't even wearing your teeth!"

"He doesn't give a damn about my teeth! He doesn't care what I look like! He just thinks about what she looks like!" Papa shouted, pointing at me.

"Didn't even wear your teeth!" Eva said as she went back to the kitchen. "What that young man must have thought of you!"

"Hmphh!" Papa answered.

On Sunday evening, when it was time for me to return to the convenience store to meet my ride home, Eva supervised Papa's attire before we were allowed to leave the apartment, and she made sure that he was wearing his teeth. He was, however, no more interested in speaking with Mitch than he had been on my arrival.

After my return to Philadelphia, I called my mother to tell her about the weekend. "Papa acted terribly to my friend!" I complained.

When I told her about it, my mother laughed. "Well, it wasn't as bad as the first time Papa met your father."

"No?"

"The first time Dad asked me out, I was 14 years old," my mother said. "My older brother brought home his friend, Jackie Lydon, and I thought Jackie was dreamy. But it was almost a year before he asked me to go to the movies with him! I was so excited! At the time, Papa was working and living in New York, so I asked my mother for permission to go to the show with Jackie. She said, 'You'll have to wait until your father comes home this weekend, and get his permission.'

"Well, when Papa got home, I told him that Pat's friend Jackie had asked me to go out to the movies, and could I go?

"'Who is this man who wants to take my little girl out on a date?' Papa asked.

"'He's not a man, Papa,' I told him. 'He's a boy at school, and he's very nice. He's a good friend of Patty's!'

"'And how old is he, Baby?' Papa asked.

"He's seventeen, Papa,' I explained.

"'Seventeen!' Papa said. 'Then he's a man. And if this man wants to take my little girl out on a date, I have to meet him before I can even think of giving my approval!'

"So Papa told me to have Jackie come over early Sunday afternoon to meet him, and we got it all arranged. But then Sunday morning, after breakfast, Papa sat down in his boxer shorts and undershirt to read the newspaper with a cup of coffee and a cigarette. And he kept reading, and kept reading, and it was getting later and later and later.

"Finally I said, 'Papa, please put on your pants!'

"And he said to me, 'Can't a man relax in his own home?'

"I said, "Please, Papa, Jackie Lydon is coming soon! Please put on your pants!'

"'I don't have to get dressed up for some young whippersnapper!' Papa said.

"Well, I begged and pleaded, but Papa just sat in the parlor in his boxers reading the paper. Finally, when it was time and your father came to the house to meet Papa and get permission to take me to the movies, I had to bring him into the parlor and introduce him to Papa who was still sitting there in his underwear! I was so embarrassed!"

"What happened then?" I asked.

"Oh, Papa grilled your father on what his intentions were, and your poor father was so shy, it was terrible for him. But then, of course, your father thought that Papa was awful to sit around like that in his undershorts in front of his daughter. But in the end, Papa finally gave his consent, provided that my brother went along too to chaperone us. Your father and I spent the next year trying to avoid my brother in the movie theater, because he and his friend used to sit behind us in the theater making kissing noises through the whole movie!"

Mitch continued to give me rides to Laurel on occasion, and eventually was permitted to drive me to the apartment instead of my having to call from the convenience store. But although Eva tried to chat and quizzed the young man when possible, Papa never favored him with much more than the occasional grunt or harrumph. To Eva's delight, Mitch and I even began dating.

"You should invite him to stay with us for the weekend!" Eva suggested.

"I don't know," I said.

"Your Poppa and I are mature adults," Eva said. "We understand that young people want to spend some time alone together. We wouldn't have any problem with that. We'd stay out of the way!"

It was a kind offer, although it was hard to imagine Papa and Eva staying quietly "out of the way." I declined; I preferred to keep Mitch's exposure to Papa limited.

Once, when Mitch and I had gone out for an evening on the town in D.C., he brought me back to Laurel after midnight, and Papa and Eva had already gone to bed. Papa was always a light sleeper and was prone to wandering the apartment during the night. I have no idea how she was able to do it, but Eva kept Papa confined in their room until after Mitch had left.

On another weekend, when Mitch came to drive me home on a Sunday evening, Papa carried my suitcase out and deposited it in Mitch's car, while I tried to keep Eva from packing as much food as she thought I'd need to bring home with me. When he came back into the apartment, Papa took me aside.

"There's a bottle of wine in that car," he informed me in whispers.

"A bottle of wine?"

"A bottle of wine!" Papa repeated. "And it's been opened! I don't like the idea of a man coming to pick you up from your grandparents' home with an open bottle of wine in the car. What kind of man does that?"

"It was probably left over from something, Papa," I said.

"I don't like it," Papa said. "Are you going to be safe? I don't want you to go with him if you won't be safe. I can take you to the train station and you can go home by train."

"I'll be fine in the car, Papa."

"I don't want him drinking with you in that car," he said.

"He won't, Papa."

"You make sure he doesn't, and you call us when you get in, and let us know you got home in one piece," he said. And of course, I did call a few hours later when I arrived safely home.

When Mitch and I stopped seeing each other, Eva was sympathetic. "Oh, that's too bad," she said.

"Too bad? Hmmmphh! Like hell!" Papa said.

"What do you mean, Hmmmphh, like hell?" Eva demanded.

"What do I mean? She's better off without him, that's what I mean!" Papa said. "I didn't trust him from the first time I saw him!"

"Well, that's just silly, Pat! How could you know anything about whether you can trust someone from just looking at him?"

Crossing his arms over his chest, Papa leaned back in his chair. "I could tell," he said. "I knew. I just knew!"

# 39

## Of Death and Divorce

Papa and I were standing together in front of Grandma's coffin, my grandmother whom I resembled, who never came to my parents' house during Papa's annual visits: Papa's first wife.

"My god!" Papa said quietly. "What happened to her hair? Did she lose her hair?"

Papa probably hadn't seen his ex-wife for close to twenty years. Although they had occasionally talked on the phone during Papa's visits to my parents' house, their last face-to-face meeting that I could remember had been when I was a little girl, several years after they divorced.

"No, Papa," I said. "She didn't lose her hair, but – "

He interrupted. "But that's a wig! Why the hell did the undertaker put a wig on her? I scarcely recognized her."

"It's her own wig, Papa. She's been wearing a wig for years."

"Whatever for?" he asked. "She had perfectly good hair!"

"She liked the wig," I said. "She thought it looked better."

"Hmmmph," he said, more softly than usual. "It's jarring! She looked fine the way she was."

My grandmother had broken her hip in a fall and subsequently suffered a heart attack. She had died while I was en route from Philadelphia to see her in the hospital. When my mother informed Papa that Grandma had died, he and Eva drove from Maryland to Massachusetts so he could be there for the services. Through two days of wake and one day of funeral Mass, burial and funeral luncheon, Papa was quiet, respectful, unobtrusive, as he encountered many people he hadn't seen in a long time,. He knelt when the situation called for it, comforted his daughter, spoke in hushed tones, chatted amiably, conversed with his children, ten of his grandchildren, and was introduced to lots of other people. If he heard them, he never acknowledged the comments of some of my grandmother's family: "What's *he* doing here? And why did he ever bring *her*?"

His Carli nephews, who were sons of Papa's brother Uncle Guido, attended the wake and funeral for Grandma. Like Papa, they were extremely short men, about five feet or under. His Carli nephews were happy to see Papa, and they spent a good bit of time chatting and catching up with him. A woman from a tall branch of Grandma's family walked past with a quizzical look on her face, and remarked to a cousin, "Where ever did they get all these little men?"

For her part, the usually gregarious Eva sat in quiet distress at the wake, remarking to me in whispers, "I just can't go into the same room where the body is. I can't help it. I can't stand to see dead bodies. I don't understand why people want to do things this way. I don't want people to come to look at me when I die! It would be horrible! And I don't want to be buried, either. Your Poppa and I want to be cremated."

It was easier when we got home after the wake. We all could get into more comfortable clothing, sit, relax. Papa and Eva were getting to know my brother Kevin's fiancee Kathy and another brother's girlfriend, both of whom were staying at my parents' home the night before the funeral. With ten of us in the small house, we were all tripping over each other.

The morning of the funeral, it was a scramble for everyone to be able to wash, get dressed and eat breakfast before leaving for the funeral parlor. As Kathy exited the bathroom, a groggy Eva was coming upstairs with towel in hand, and I was heading to the stairs to go down to the kitchen. Looking up in surprise at Kathy, Eva demanded, *"Who* are *you?"*

"I'm Kathy," came the answer.

"Kathy?" Eva echoed. "I didn't recognize you! You don't look at all the same when you're not wearing your glasses!" She gave Kathy a long stare, and then took her turn in the bathroom.

"Did she think I broke into the house?" Kathy whispered to me. "I don't know why she didn't recognize me. I've been spending time with her for the last two days.

At the funeral later that morning, in the front row just to the right of the center aisle sat Papa, then Eva, me, my mother, my father, my uncle. When I returned to the pew after doing a reading that my mother had asked me to do for the funeral, Eva leaned close and put a hand on my shoulder. "I don't understand this at all," she said. "Your Poppa and I never have anything to do with religion. It's all mumbo jumbo to us."

The next time that I visited them in Maryland, Eva left me to talk with Papa while she went on an errand. He and I sat at the kitchen table, coffee mugs in hand, more coffee on low heat on the stove should we need it.

"I want you to know something," Papa told me. "I want you to know that your grandmother was never anything other than what she had always promised to be. She didn't change at all. It was I who changed, not she, I who wanted something different. There I was, a young married man, teaching in Buffalo, a wife, two little children, and I was miserable. I wanted something else. I didn't know what to do. I was so desperate that I even went to a priest for help. Me! A nonbeliever!

I went to a priest! What the hell I ever thought he could do to help, I don't know! What could he tell me? What did he know about it? But I was desperate!"

"What did he tell you, Papa?" I asked.

"He told me what they have to say. He told me to stay with my wife. He told me to try harder. I did. I tried. I tried. But it didn't work. I had changed, and I couldn't change back. Your grandmother and I argued and argued and argued. We were both miserable. And we made the children miserable." He closed his eyes.

"During the war, when I was with the USO, you know I spent a year in Brazil. I sent money home regularly for Evelyn and the children. That whole year, she scrimped and saved. I didn't know it; I sent plenty of money, but they lived on next to nothing, and when I came back from Brazil, she told me she had saved the money for a down payment so that we could buy a house. A house! It was the last thing in the world I wanted, and she knew it. I had been asking for a divorce for years.

"I was a bastard. Plain and simple. I was a bastard. But I couldn't keep living with her anymore. I found work in New York. She and the children stayed in Massachusetts. I came to Massachusetts for weekends from time to time.

"Divorce laws were different then. In order to get a divorce in those days, you had to prove fault. I gave her cause; lord knows I gave her cause, but she didn't want the divorce, and she wouldn't initiate it. I begged her for years, but she wanted the marriage. What marriage did we have? It was a sham! But she wanted the marriage.

"I finally sued her for divorce on the grounds of desertion. By then the children were grown, your mother was married, and you were a baby. I told the judge I had employment in New York, and my wife wouldn't come to live with me there. It was a lie. Of course it wasn't she who had deserted me. I had long before deserted her. I begged her, just say nothing, don't answer the charge of desertion, let me go. I'll pay alimony, just let the divorce take place. I wore her down, and she finally gave in. So not only were we divorced, but legally speaking, the divorce was blamed on her. I was a bastard." He paused. "I just wanted you to know, she remained the person she had always promised to be. It was I who had changed." He took off his glasses and wiped them on his napkin.

"Do you want some more coffee, Papa?" I asked.

"Coffee?" He peered into his mug. "I think I do need more coffee! And where did Eva put my racing paper? There's a horse I'm keeping an eye on, great parentage, good performance in the early runs, but I have my doubts about the jockey."

Later, after Eva returned from her errands, Papa retired to his den to study his racing papers while I helped her get things together for lunch.

"You know," Eva said as she put the bread out, "I'm not the kind of person who would ever want to break up a marriage."

"I know, Eva," I said.

"Your Poppa and your grandmother already had problems and weren't living together when your Poppa and I fell in love. But I didn't want to be responsible for a family breaking up. I'm not that kind of person. I told him that he had to go back to his family and try to make it work. And he did go back, but it didn't work. And then she just wouldn't give him the divorce. I hated it those years. But I never wanted to hurt anyone."

"I know," I said.

Papa appeared in the kitchen doorway, racing paper in hand. "What happened to lunch?" he asked.

Eva sighed one of her deep, long sighs.

"What is it, darling?" he asked.

She sighed again. "Well, I'm just thinking about all the things I have to do this afternoon, Pat. I'm going to make chicken parmesan for dinner tonight, and I have to get a chiffon cake into the oven before I make dinner."

"Fine, fine," Papa said. "But let's eat lunch first!"

# 40

# Dinner with Jimmy

"We're going to Jimmy's for dinner tonight," Eva said. "He and your Poppa are old friends."

"Jimmy's a character," Papa said. "I first met him just after I started to work for the Department of Health, Education and Welfare."

"Before we lived in Laurel," Eva added. "Right after we moved to the District."

"Papa, what did you do at HEW?"

"Worked on setting up guidance departments in high schools," Papa said. "It was a big change from the way things had been done up to that point. Different approach to career guidance."

"Your Poppa traveled all over doing that."

"I did some travelling. I was working on developing and implementing the model for guidance departments. It was related to the National Defense Education Act. That's part of what I did. And I worked on setting up the student loan program under the Act."

"I had NDEA loans when I went to Clark," I said.

"Good program," Papa said.

"Did you like the work at HEW, Papa?"

"The guidance work – that was interesting. I met some good people, bright people, people with ideas. Corresponded with some of them for years. But, later, some of the time, I was pushing paper. Couldn't wait to retire then! Get home, do whatever I like, put my feet up, read as much as I want! Retirement suits me."

When we arrived at Jimmy's home for dinner on that warm summer evening, our host was eager to show us his vegetable garden. "Look at those tomatoes, Pat!" he said, pointing to the plants heavy with beefsteak tomatoes.

"*Those* are tomatoes! Just smell them!" Papa exclaimed. "You can't get a good tomato in the supermarket these days. The stuff they sell has no taste, no taste at all."

"Oh, Pat, wait until you taste these!" Jimmy said. He was a husky tall man with a booming voice, an ever-present smile, and a gregarious manner; he towered over Papa, Eva and me. His wife was just as welcoming and friendly as he, and we had a delightful evening with them.

"You know how your grandfather and I met?" Jimmy asked me over dinner.

"You worked together at HEW?" I said.

Papa raised an eyebrow and stared at me quizzically, but Jimmy just laughed. "No, it was Pat who worked at HEW. I had a news stand nearby. One morning, this little guy with a little mustache, wearing glasses, dressed in a suit, came up to me at the counter, and he had a paper in his hand. He said to me, 'Glad to see you have the racing paper. I'll take this one, and I want you to save one for me from now on! I'll be in to pick it up!'

"I told him, 'The racing paper goes fast, so if you want one, you'd better make sure you get in early. I don't save anything for anyone.'

"Well, this little tough guy with the mustache, the glasses and the suit, he looked up at me, and he said, 'I don't give a goddamn what you do for anyone else, but you're going to save one for me!'" Jimmy laughed again.

"So what happened?" I asked.

"What else could I do? I saved one for him the next time, and and the next time, and we became friends."

In the car on the way home, I said, "That was such a nice time! Papa, I can see why you've kept in touch with Jimmy all these years after you retired."

"Of course we kept in touch," Papa said. "He was my bookie!"

"Your bookie, Papa?"

"For years."

"The bookie who used to call you when you visited at our house when I was a kid?"

"Yes, that was Jimmy. He's not a bookie anymore. Ran into some tax trouble with the government a few years back, and he managed to get out of it, but he had to give up the business. Now he grows tomatoes."

# 41

## Papa and Door-to-Door Religion

On the wall of their living room, right next to the front door, Papa and Eva had a large, framed piece of art that Papa loved, and it always puzzled me, since Papa so hated religion. The bulk of the watercolor was a representation of a large body of water, perhaps an ocean. Toward the bottom right, there was a rough sketch of a tiny man in a tiny boat. In the upper left these words were written: *Oh, Lord, thy sea is so vast, and my boat is so small.*

*   *      *

One Saturday after lunch, Eva and I were at the front door, just about to leave for some afternoon errands, when we were startled by a knock. "Whoever could that be?" Eva said. She opened the door to three young men neatly dressed in suits and ties who smiled, and asked if they could speak with us.

"I'm sorry. We're just going out," Eva said.

Papa's den was just opposite the front door. Leaving his racing papers, he poked his head out. "What's this?" he asked.

One of the young men stepped forward and handed Papa a religious pamphlet. "We're visiting people in your apartment building to talk about the good news of Jesus Christ."

"Come in! Come in!" Papa said. "I'd love to hear your beliefs, and I have some questions for you!"

"Yes, sir," the young man said. "We'd be glad to answer your questions."

*Invite them in?* I thought. *Oh, no! I'd been no more than polite to members of a similar group who came to my door one time, and they came back every month for a year!*

"Kay and I will be out for an hour or so, Pat," Eva said.

"Fine, fine." As we closed the door behind us, I could hear Papa addressing the young men. "Let's sit in the kitchen. Do you take coffee?"

When Eva and I returned an hour and a half later, Papa barely gave us a nod. He and the young men had moved their conversation from the kitchen to the living room, and they were all standing.

"Now, the next question I have – " Papa said.

"Sir, we really have to go," one fellow said. The three young men were shifting from foot to foot, backs to the wall, edging toward the front door.

"There are several issues we've barely touched upon!" Papa protested.

"But we haven't had time to visit any of the other apartments," a second fellow said.

"Oh, Pat," Eva said, "you've bothered them long enough, and I have to start dinner soon!"

"Bothered them? I'm not bothering them! I'm interested in how they explain the contradictions between their religious beliefs and the fact that religions have been responsible for most of the wars in the entire history of the world! "

"Well, you'll just have to ask them some other time, Pat, because they said they need to go!"

The tallest young fellow managed to get his hand on the doorknob. "Yes, sir, it's getting late, and our ride will be leaving."

"Well, the next time you come to our building, make sure you stop by," Papa said. "We've hardly scratched the surface!"

"Yes, sir. Thank you, sir."

The three backed out the door, and made good their escape.

"Hmmmph," Papa said.

"Did you see how fast they dashed out?" Eva said. "I don't expect they'll be back,"

"Doubtful, doubtful," Papa said. "Hmmmph! You know, they don't take coffee."

# 42

# Managing Melon

Papa had stopped going to the racetrack, but he still bought the racing paper regularly. One Saturday morning, he went out after our lengthy breakfast to pick up a racing paper and returned about an hour later, with the paper to be sure, but also carrying a large melon. "Eva! Eva! Look what I got!" he called as he came from the garden into their living room. "The Giant was having a sale on honeydew!"

Eva, who had been watering her jungle of houseplants near the sliding glass doors, looked up in dismay. "Oh, Pat! What on earth am I going to do with that?"

"What are *you* going to *do* with it?" Papa asked. "I don't care about what *you* do with it! *I'm* going to eat it!"

"Let me see it!" She grabbed the melon out of his hands, tapped it, shook it, and sniffed at it. "Pat, this melon is ripe!" she said accusingly. "We'll have to use it right away!"

"Of course it's ripe, darling," Papa said, grabbing it back from her. "I know how to pick a ripe melon! It's perfect! I'm going to cut a piece right now!"

"Darn it, Pat! I just finished cleaning the kitchen!" Eva said. "I haven't even had time to get dressed yet!"

"I don't know what you're talking about!" Papa said. "Get dressed whenever you want! Change your clothing a dozen times if you like! I can cut a melon myself!"

"You'll make a mess of everything!" she complained. "And who will put it away? I can't imagine where we'll put it!"

"She can't imagine where we'll put it!" Papa boomed. "We'll put it in the refrigerator! Where else would we put it?"

"He has no idea of the problems he causes!" Eva told me, as they moved the argument into the kitchen.

"The problems I cause!" Papa placed the melon on the kitchen table. "I bring her a beautiful melon, and I'm causing problems!"

"Every time he goes to the Giant, he does this!" Eva opened the pantry door. "Look at all the stewed tomatoes we have! He bought twelve cans last week!"

"They were on sale!" Papa said. "It was a bargain! You don't have to use them all at once!"

"I had to stack them on the pantry floor! Now I don't have enough room for anything else!" she muttered. "I can't imagine where I'll put that melon!"

Papa, meanwhile, had got out the big wooden cutting board, a large knife and was reaching for plates. "Who wants some melon?" he asked.

"You'll spoil your appetite for lunch!" Eva said, as he began slicing into the melon.

"None for me right now," I said.

"Just cut me a little piece, Pat," Eva told him. "Well, a little bigger than that!"

But after they finished the melon snack, the real challenge was on. When Eva opened the refrigerator, it didn't seem possible that any more food could be stored therein. "Oh, darn!" she said. "I'll have to repack something!"

She pulled out several containers and jammed their contents into still smaller containers, rearranged two shelves, and began slicing and wrapping the remaining melon. I can't say how she did it, but she managed to fit every bit of melon into that overstuffed refrigerator, although she did push melon at every meal that weekend.

I never saw their refrigerator when it wasn't packed to the gills. Eva would always choose the smallest possible container in which to pack any leftover, and she never threw away a thing, even if that caused her to have to eat another forkful or two of whatever she was putting away. She had a vast store of containers and odd jars which I would have to reach down from a shelf for her after meals. No matter that there didn't seem to be a smidgeon of empty space in that refrigerator! Eva would magically manage to fit in still more food.

# 43

# Of Bananas and Spots

As we sat for breakfast one Saturday morning, Eva brandished a piece of a banana. "Does anyone want the other half of my banana? I only use half on my bran."

"No, thanks," I said.

"They're very good bananas," Eva encouraged, sliding it toward me.

"Hah!" Papa said. "Neither of you has any idea what a banana really tastes like!"

Eva shook her head. "Of course I know what it tastes like, Pat!"

Papa reached for the abandoned half and sniffed it. "This smells nothing at all like a banana! It isn't even ripe!"

"This banana certainly is ripe, Pat!" Eva said. "It smells the way they always do, and it's perfectly sweet!"

"Sweet!" Papa said. "You don't know what you're talking about! Bananas ripen only on the tree, and the taste of a fresh, ripe banana – you couldn't begin to understand unless you've had one!"

"That's just nonsense! Bananas don't have to be on a tree to ripen," she muttered. "Sometimes I buy green bananas and let them ripen at home in a brown paper bag!"

"A brown paper bag!" Papa roared. "You don't have any idea of what a ripe banana tastes like until you've had one fresh from the tree! When I was in Brazil with the USO during the war, we'd have bananas, freshly picked! They'd cut them down in huge bunches! I'd never seen anything like it! Huge bunches! And the taste of those bananas! You have no idea! Those – *those!* – were bananas! These days bananas are picked green, they are shipped green, and they sit for days before you get them. They never get ripe!"

"They do too get ripe!" Eva said. "They turn yellow!"

"You know nothing about it. Those bananas you get at the store aren't anything at all like what we had in Brazil!" Papa scooped a heaping spoon of oatmeal from his bowl and brought it to his mouth.

"He's always going on like this! But, Pat, that reminds me; you should tell Kay about your check-up last week," she said. "Kay, you know we see Dr. Kirschner. He's a top man!"

"Hmmmph," Papa said. "Kirschner likes to keep an eye on me. There's that spot on my lung, you see."

"A spot on your lung, Papa?" I asked. It was news to me.

"Damn strangest thing," he said. "It showed up on an X-ray a few years back. When Kirschner told me about it, I thought, all those years I smoked, there it goes, lung cancer. But he tells me, it's not lung cancer. 'It's a fungus,' he says to me. I couldn't believe it! 'A fungus?' I ask him. 'How the hell did I get a fungus in my lung?'"

"Tell her the whole story, Pat," Eva said.

Papa took off his glasses and leaned back in his chair. "That's what I'm doing, darling! That's what I'm doing! So, Kirschner tells me that it's a fungus common to turtles. 'Have you spent much time around turtles?' he asks me. Have I spent much time around turtles! 'Hell, no!' I tell him. Well, he begins to quiz me, one question, and another, and another, and what it finally comes down to is he thinks I contracted it in Brazil during the Second World War!"

"Were you around turtles in Brazil, Papa?" I asked.

"Turtles? Hell, no! We don't know how I picked it up, but Kirschner's best guess is that I got it when I was in Brazil."

"And you've had a fungus in your lungs all this time?"

"That's what he thinks. Hmmmph," Papa said. "So he keeps an eye on it. A fungus! It's the damnedest thing!"

"When did they find it, Papa?"

"Oh, it's been a few years. Didn't change much for a long time, but it's giving me a little trouble now."

"Didn't they treat it when they first found it?" I asked.

"Didn't need to; wasn't bothering me. Kirschner has me on theophilline now," Papa said. "Helps me breathe. I looked it up. Coffee, tea, chocolate – they all contain a chemical that acts as a stimulant, but each is different. The stimulant in tea is much stronger than the one in coffee. Much stronger! Totally different thing! Theophilline is derived from tea."

"And now I have to give your Poppa therapy at home too," Eva said.

"You do?" I asked.

"Every day."

"What kind of therapy?"

"Kirschner showed me what to do. Your Poppa lies down, and then I cup my hands like this," Eva demonstrated, "and I drum on your Poppa's back with my cupped hands."

"Eva's got it down perfectly. Perfectly!"

"It helps, then?"

"It breaks up the congestion," Eva explained.

"Eva has to rest afterwards," Papa said.

"It's very taxing," she agreed. "I do it for fifteen minutes at a time."

"But it helps," Papa said.

"It does," Eva said.

"She's a godsend!"

"Oh, Pat!" Eva smiled as she reached for the banana half. "Kay, you pour more coffee for us. As soon as I wrap the rest of this banana, I'll put the rum buns out!"

"Rum buns! That's more like it. Now, rum buns are sweet, darling! But not half as sweet as – "

"Don't you start again on those bananas, Pat!"

Papa paused, then leaned forward and cupped Eva's face with both his hands. "Not half as sweet as you, darling!"

# 44

## Cancer

It was my mother on the phone. "I have terrible news! Papa has lung cancer!"

"No, it's not cancer. He has a fungus in his lung," I said. "He's had it for a long time."

"I don't know anything about a fungus. Eva called me, and she says he has cancer," Mum said.

"What did Papa say about it?" I asked.

"Eva called me when Papa wasn't home, because he doesn't know. She says that the doctor thinks it's better not to tell him."

"Papa would want to know! He's not the kind of person who wants to be kept in the dark! " I said. "They have to tell him!"

*   *   *

I visited the next weekend.

"I suppose you've heard," Papa said. "Lung cancer. If something else doesn't get me first, I'll die of it."

"Oh, Papa," I said.

"I've decided to take radiation treatments. The side effects aren't bad, and it could shrink the tumor. I'm not going to take chemotherapy. I've known people who tried that, and what it did to them – well, I'm not willing to do it. Kirschner told me they can't do surgery. That's the bad news. But there's good news."

"What's the good news?" I asked.

"The good news is that I'm 81. When you're 81, the body slows down. Digestion isn't as fast, and when you cut yourself, your body can't repair itself as quickly. But it turns out that when you're 81 years old, cancer cells can't grow as quickly either. Kirschner says I could live with it for quite some time."

"Well, that's good."

"Eva! Do we have any more coffee?"

"I'll get it," Eva said. "Just a minute!"

Papa slid his glasses lower on his nose, and looked over the rims at me. "So," he said, "what can you tell me? What's the news from Pennsylvania?"

* * * *

Birthday card from Eva and Papa, signed only by Eva:

Dear Kay: We do both wish you so many good wishes for your birthday. I would have liked to have gone off and picked out a "something" that was an exciting gift on opening, but a gift certificate was the best I (we) could do, and considering it was likely to reach you in time. Sure hope it did.

For Papa -- some days are good and some aren't. When you come down we can talk about it more if you like, but obviously he is so involved with analysis of self, etc., but what he feels is a depletion of himself, and so he's angry most of the time, unhappily, I think, -- we think. But today is an up day for him for which I'm always glad -- and selfishly, then, for me too! Have fun, Kay, with the family when you're home and a wonderful birthday time, now and always. We do send our love and the best of wishes to all.

~ Eva and Papa

* * * *

"Your Poppa is going to drive me crazy!" Eva said. "He keeps a clipboard and a little notebook at the table, and every time he eats or drinks something, he writes it down, every little thing. It's crazy! It's absolutely crazy! Why would a person *do* something like that?"

"He wants to make sure he eats enough, Eva."

"I always give him plenty to eat! It's just nonsense!"

"It's because of the cancer, Eva. He's trying to get lots of food in and keep his weight up to help his body fight it."

"I give him lots of food! I always give him lots of food! He doesn't need to write it down."

"It helps him. Keeping the record helps him see that he's fighting it, Eva."

130

"Is that why he does it? Hmmm. Well, I'll try not to say anything about it, then, but it's very irritating."

* * * *

Papa brought the mail to the kitchen table. "Your mother has sent me something," he told me.

"She's been sending mail to your Poppa every day," Eva said. "What is it today, Pat?"

Papa slit the envelope and pulled out a collection of clippings and notes. "Oh, look, darling, Evie sent a photo of a kitten."

"Let me see! Oh, look at it, Pat! Isn't it just darling!"

"And your father's sent me some clippings from the editorial page," he told me. "Jackie and I send each other good columns we come across."

"Aren't there any jokes today?" Eva asked. "Evie usually sends some jokes."

"Elephant jokes! Ha! It's the damnedest thing! Why does an elephant lie on its back with its feet in the air?"

"Why?" I asked.

"To trip small birds!" Papa chuckled.

"She sends the silliest jokes!" Eva said. "And what about cartoons? Are there any cartoons today?"

"Yes, darling, there are cartoons. Dagwood and Blondie, of course, and Charlie Brown."

* * * *

Papa and I were sitting at the kitchen table, talking together for the hour or two it would take Eva to get dressed.

"Eva can't talk about death," Papa told me.

I remembered her reluctance to be in the same room with a dead body at my grandmother's wake. "Hmmm," I said.

"She's afraid of death; so afraid she can't talk about it, or even think about it. And there are things she needs to know. I try to talk to her about our finances, so she'll know what she needs to know, and how to manage things when she's on her own, but she refuses to discuss it. She won't listen. She can't face death."

"I'm sorry, Papa."

"She's always been like that. Can't look the thing in the face. It's a damned shame, but she can't do it."

* * * *

"Your Poppa is so down!" Eva said. "He likes talking to you. Why don't you talk to him? I'll go out and leave the two of you alone."

* * * *

Papa and I sat at the kitchen table, each with a mug of coffee.

"Do you think you're depressed, Papa?" I asked.

He shrugged, folded his arms. "Maybe. Maybe a tad depressed."

"It might help to have someone you could talk to about things, Papa. The cancer's a hard thing to deal with. There's no shame in talking with someone."

He looked into my face, then closed his eyes. "I think I told you once about when I went into therapy years ago after a health problem. I had always been healthy, and then, suddenly, I wasn't. Couldn't accept it. Fought against it. The therapist told me I was banging my head against a brick wall, and I could bang it as long as I wanted, but I couldn't knock down that brick wall. The thing is, I'm up against another brick wall, and I know I'm banging my head against the damned wall, but I'm not ready yet to stop banging my head." He shook his head. "I may need to talk with someone at some point later. May. Don't believe that right now I need to."

"Okay, Papa."

"I thank you for talking to me about it, though, and I'll think about it. I'll think about it."

# 45

# Surprise for Christmas

"How was your Christmas?" Eva asked. She and Papa both knew I had been in Massachusetts at my parents' home for the holiday.

"Oh, it was great," I said.

"What did you get for Christmas?" she asked.

"I got some good books," I said.

"Did you get any *special* gifts?" she asked.

"Special gifts?" I blushed and fumbled for words. I still couldn't imagine what had possessed my mother this year. On Christmas, when I saw what it was, I hadn't wanted to display her gift in front of my father and brothers, and I certainly did not want to talk about it with my grandfather either. "What do you mean?"

"Well, didn't you like the negligee?" Eva demanded.

All too fresh was my memory of Christmas morning, when I'd opened one box with a tag that read "Love, Mum and Dad."

My father, who usually had no idea what my mother had purchased for any of us kids until after the gift was unwrapped, had asked me, "What is it?"

"A nightgown," I'd said, trying to sound normal, as I slammed the box lid back over the gift inside: silky, slinky, sexy, lacy, spaghetti-strapped, low-cut, and bright red.

But what to say now to Eva? "It was fine," I said, hoping to change the subject.

"Your mom told me what she was trying to find for you," Eva said. "I thought it was a great idea! We talked about it, and we both thought you might not have something like that. It could make a difference with the fellow you're seeing."

"Damn fools, you and Evie, both of you! Kay doesn't need something like that! A man will love her for who she is, not for some damn, stupid, cheap little thing like that!"

"It wasn't cheap at all, Pat! Evie got it at a top department store! She sent me pictures, and it was very nice!"

"The two of you, calling each other back and forth, sending pictures, is this one better, is that one better! I told you, you sounded like you're running a meat market! Something like that would cheapen her! She's not like that!" Papa roared.

"That's just foolish, Pat! We're all mature adults!"

"Mature adults, hell! She doesn't need to parade herself in front of some damn man like that!" He took off his glasses and looked me in the eye. "I tell you, I had nothing to do with it! I was against it from the start!"

# 46

## Important Errands

"Kay, I need you to pick up a few things for me at the Giant," Eva said.

"Sure, Eva. What do you need?"

"I want a tomato for the salad tonight." She sighed. "Pick out a big one, very red, a little soft, but not too soft."

"You can't get good tomatoes anymore," Papa said. "They don't have any taste."

"Don't start about tomatoes, Pat."

"What did I say?" Papa asked. "I said you can't get good tomatoes, and you can't! They're like mush."

"Kay is going to get a good tomato!"

"Hmmmph. There's no such thing as a good tomato anymore. Not unless you grow your own."

"Don't pay any attention to him," Eva said. "Get a tomato, no, get two. I'll need to cut some slices for sandwiches for lunch, so try to be quick. We need a bottle of the diet cola too. Don't get any of those fancy ones. The store brand tastes perfectly fine."

"We drink it all the time," Papa said.

"And your Poppa takes a dietary supplement now."

"It's a milkshake."

"To keep his weight up," Eva added.

"It's delicious!"

"I want you to get three cans."

"Get the vanilla," Papa said.

"I know there was something else." Eva opened the refrigerator door and studied the contents.

"While you're out," Papa said, "I want you to pick up something for me. Do you remember the store where I go to get my racing paper?"

I had been there with him many times. "Yes, Papa."

"I'd like you to get me my racing paper."

"Sure, Papa."

"Brown sugar, that was it! Oh, I'll write you a list!" Eva took a small pad of paper from the counter and sat down at the kitchen table. "I have that ham to bake for dinner tonight, and I'll need more brown sugar for the coating. The dark brown sugar, not the light! Get two boxes."

"Okay."

"And my racing paper," Papa added.

"And I need you to pick up my green jacket from the dry cleaner."

"Sure," I said.

"And my racing paper."

"And remember the lamp shop I took you to?" Eva asked. "They called and said that the hobnail milk glass chimney I ordered has come in. Could you pick that up too?"

"No problem."

"Don't forget my racing paper!"

"Let me just go get my bag, and I'll get the dry cleaning slip for you." Eva hurried off to their bedroom.

Papa tore off a scrap of paper from a newspaper, and placed his left hand to guard it almost as if he were a schoolboy afraid someone might steal the correct test answers from him. Leaning over the paper, he began to write.

"I found it," Eva announced. "Here's the slip from the cleaner, and here's the money, and here's the list."

Papa glanced up, then underlined some of what he had written, and folded the paper into a tiny package, which he handed to me. "Here's my list. You can read it later."

As soon as I got into my car, I opened Papa's folded paper and smiled. This is what it said:

Get my papers (<u>of course</u>)

Get whatever else you can --

if you can, when it be had

quickly -- <u>if it can</u>!

But ... otherwise

Get my papers!

COME HOME

TEAR THIS UP

<u>SAY WHAT YOU WILL</u>

# 47

## Andy and the Chicken Parmesan

Eva and I came back from the Giant one afternoon to find Papa and a man I didn't know sitting at the kitchen table, poring over a racing paper. On our arrival, Papa's friend jumped to his feet.

"Could I help you carry anything in, Eva?" he asked.

"Oh, hello, Andy," Eva said. "No, that's everything." We put our grocery bags on the counter.

"Andy," Papa said, "this is my granddaughter, Kay. She's my daughter's oldest."

Still standing, Andy smiled and nodded at me. "Pleased to meet you."

"Andy's come over to ask my advice on the matter of a horse," Papa told me.

"No one knows more about horses than the Professor," Andy said.

"Sit down, Andy," Eva said.

He nodded again, and took his seat.

As I helped Eva put the groceries away, Papa and Andy resumed their discussion. "Well, of course you know that this horse's parentage raises some questions," Papa said. "The dam is solid! Couldn't ask for more! But the sire – Hmmmph!"

"But didn't he win his first time out, Professor?" Andy said.

"He did. But he was damned inconsistent after that! Don't forget!" Papa launched into a recitation of the triumphs and failings of the horse's father.

"So, not worth it?" Andy sounded discouraged.

"We can't say yet. *Why* was the sire so inconsistent? That's the question! " Papa said. "Now if you consider *his* parentage!" Papa expounded on the family tree of the sire, followed by discourse on odd members of the dam's family, topped by a lecture on jockeys and their styles. I didn't know what Andy was making of it, but my head was spinning!

"Pat!" Eva interrupted. "I'm putting on some coffee."

"Don't trouble yourself, Eva," Andy said. "You don't need to do that!"

"Well, you'll drink some, won't you?" Eva demanded.

"Of course he'll drink some coffee, darling," Papa said. "We'll all have some! But Andy and I don't need to know anything else about it until it's ready!" And he went back to horse talk, examining in turn the ancestry of each horse competing in a given race, as well as the history of the jockeys.

"Kay, get out the rum buns, and those cookies you brought too," Eva said. "And get some mugs, and the new beleek tea cup for my tea."

I got out the mugs and tea cup, and spoons and plates all around. When the hot drinks were ready, I put the plate of goodies on the table, while Eva poured her tea and the coffee.

"Have a rum bun, Andy," she encouraged.

"Just coffee for me please, Eva," Andy said.

Papa grabbed a large cookie from the plate before pushing it aside. "We won't need all this!" Turning back to Andy, he continued, "Now, where things really get interesting – you remember who else this trainer worked with?"

Eva took her tea cup and a piece of rum bun to the counter with her. "I'm going to get started on making dinner!" she said.

Andy turned to her and smiled. "Good coffee," he said. "Thanks, Eva."

"Do you need help, Eva?" I asked.

"Not now," she answered. "You just sit and have your coffee and visit with your Poppa and Andy while I get things started."

Papa and Andy switched from racing papers to Papa's carefully maintained notebooks, in which he recorded information about horses, races and jockeys, and back to newspapers again. They didn't pay the slightest attention to Eva and me, but I found it fascinating to watch their deliberations.

"I see what you mean, Professor," Andy said quietly, as he studied one page of Papa's copious notes.

"Andy!" Eva's voice was loud, sharp and demanding, and Andy jumped.

"Yes, Eva?" he answered.

"Andy! What is your wife making for dinner tonight?"

"For dinner tonight? I don't know what she's making for dinner tonight, Eva. We might go out."

"Well, where are you going?"

"Where are they going," Papa muttered.

"I don't know, Eva. Sometimes we go out on the weekend. Nothing fancy. "

"Well, we're staying home," Eva said. "I'm making chicken parmesan! Does your wife ever make chicken parmesan?"

"Chicken parmesan? I don't know. When we have chicken, she usually roasts it or fries it, I think."

"Well, I like to make chicken parmesan. I use boneless breasts, and when I bread them, I use the Italian bread crumbs. After I bread the chicken breasts, I fry them in olive oil first, and put them in the oven later. Does your wife ever do that?" Eva asked.

"I don't know, Eva," Andy said.

"Well, it's a very good way to prepare chicken! You should tell her to try it."

"Fine, fine, fine!" Papa said. "We're trying to talk about horses here!"

"I was just telling Andy about chicken recipes, Pat."

"Andy and I don't give a goddamn about chicken recipes!"

"You know you love my chicken parmesan!"

"Of course I love your chicken parmesan! Everyone loves your chicken parmesan! But we don't need to know the goddamn recipe!"

"Well, I just wanted to know if his wife prepared chicken the same way I do!"

"I don't know," Andy repeated nervously.

"Darling, what the hell would Andy know about how his wife prepares chicken?"

"Well, he might know."

"He might know! Hah! He doesn't know a goddamn thing about it!"

"Andy, after I fry it," Eva said, "I put the chicken in the baking dish. You need to grease the baking dish first. Then I cover the chicken with tomato sauce. I always use some oregano and a little sugar in the sauce. A little sugar makes everything better."

"A little sugar," Papa echoed, shaking his head.

"And then I put fontina cheese on top."

"She puts fontina cheese on top!" Papa announced. "Fontina! What about the parmesan?"

"Fontina is much better than parmesan, Pat. I sprinkle on some parmesan, but only a little parmesan!"

"Only a little parmesan! You got that, Andy? Only a little parmesan! Only a little! And I'm still trying to talk about horses!"

"Well, go back to your horses, Pat!" Eva said. "I was only making conversation with Andy about how his wife cooks chicken! Tell her she can call me any time about the chicken parmesan, Andy. It's a very good recipe."

Andy and Papa talked a little longer, but soon Andy gathered up his papers and said he needed to get home. "Thanks for your help, Professor," he said. "It was nice to meet you, Kay. And thank you for the coffee, Eva."

"Don't forget to tell your wife about the chicken parmesan!" Eva said.

"Don't worry," Andy said. "I'll be sure to tell her all about it."

"The goddamn chicken parmesan," Papa muttered.

# 48

## A Little Stroke

I answered the phone on a Thursday night to a call from Eva. "Your Poppa wanted me to let you know," she said, "he's had something like a little stroke."

"A stroke! Is he all right?" I asked.

"It was just a little one. They didn't even call it a stroke. They called it a cardiovascular accident, just an accident. He's fine," she said. "The doctor said he'll be back to normal in a few days."

"What hospital is he in?"

"They didn't keep him at the hospital!" Eva said. "They sent him home. It's really nothing, but your Poppa thought you should be told. You know how he is."

"What happened?" I asked.

"It was the strangest thing. Your Poppa couldn't talk for a little while."

"Papa couldn't talk?" It was almost inconceivable!

"Just for a few hours. He can talk now."

"Could I speak to him?" I asked.

"It's hard to understand him. He doesn't want to talk on the phone yet."

"If it's all right, Eva, I'll come for the weekend."

"Well, he'll love that! We always love to have you visit, but you shouldn't worry. Your Poppa's doing fine, and it's really not a problem."

"I'll come tomorrow, Eva."

I left straight from work the next day, and arrived after dark. As usual, Papa and Eva had waited dinner for me. Eva bustled around the stove with last minute preparations, and Papa sat at the kitchen table, hands around the coffee mug I'd given him.

"Good to see you," Papa said. His voice was quieter, his words were a little slurred, and one side of his mouth was drooping just a bit. "Good of you to come."

I hugged him, relieved to get one of those sloppy kisses I'd dreaded as a child. "How are you, Papa?"

He shrugged.

"He's fine," Eva said. "You know you're fine, Pat."

"Hmmmph! I'm fine, she says."

"Kirschner says you'll be better in no time!" Eva said. "I can't see why you make a big thing of it!"

"Why I make a big thing of it. Hell! You have no idea, darling! No idea at all!"

"It's just foolishness!"

"Hell!"

"See?" Eva said to me. "It's nothing, and that's the way he acts about it."

"She thinks it's nothing," Papa muttered. "Nothing."

After breakfast on Saturday, Eva left Papa and me to talk together.

"Damn thing, that stroke," he said.

"It is."

"I couldn't speak! Couldn't say a word! I was so afraid! My whole life has been about talking. And to be unable to speak! Unable to communicate! Still alive and unable to say a damn thing! I'd rather die. I'd rather die."

"Oh, Papa."

"All my life, I've been a gadfly. Socrates said he was a gadfly in the service of truth. He tried to keep them honest. I speak out. Always spoke out. *The emperor has no clothes.* Truths. Inconvenient truths."

I nodded, thinking of his calls to the White House to complain.

"And to be unable to talk!" He paused. "My speech isn't clear. Don't know if others can understand me."

"I can understand you, Papa. Your speech is a little slurred, but it's understandable."

"The doctor says it'll get better," he said. "Should improve."

"Maybe it just takes some time, Papa. You're not slurring much. You're understandable now."

"I didn't know how I could bear it if I lost the ability to speak. Most frightening thing in the world. I'd rather die."

I touched his hand.

"Hmmm," he said, looking into his coffee mug.

"You want some more coffee, Papa?

"I think I need another cup," he said.

I refilled his mug, and was turning back to the stove to put the percolator back on the burner, when he spoke. "My nose is big, but I don't need that much room for it. Fill the mug up all the way!"

I laughed. "Okay, Papa."

"And hand me that paper on the step stool, will you? I saved a column for you, thought you'd like it. The fellow's a damn fine writer! He always says what he thinks!"

# 49

## Someone Special

That was March.

In April, I met a guy, someone special, but a special guy who lived 40 miles away from me. After our first date, we talked on the phone most nights, and got together once a week. Thus busily occupied, I didn't drive down to Maryland as often. In mid-May, the special fellow proposed, I accepted, and we set the wedding date for late August, when we would be married in Massachusetts, near where I had grown up.

When I called Papa and Eva to tell them, they were happy, excited, and wanted to meet the fellow. I promised that we would come down to see them before the wedding.

"We won't be able to go to the wedding," Eva said. "Your Poppa isn't well enough for that."

It was not a surprise. Two of my brothers had married during the year preceding, and Papa, then preparing for radiation treatments, had been unable to attend their weddings. Although I wished that things could be otherwise, I understood. "Don't worry," I told Eva. "There will be lots of pictures, and I'll tell you and Papa all about it when we get back."

Although I kept Papa and Eva up-to-date by way of phone calls, it was June before I brought Tom to Laurel to meet them. I expected the usual pattern of spending most of the time around the kitchen table, drinking coffee and eating too much. Surprisingly, while we did have some table time, we spent a good bit of a Sunday afternoon sitting in their living room, talking with them in an almost formal tone. Eva presented me with their gift of a giant cookbook chock-full of haute cuisine. She expected that I would need to entertain frequently, and wanted me to be well-prepared. It was a lovely cookbook.

Papa looked a bit frail – thinner and smaller – but he had recovered quite a bit from his stroke. His speech was mostly clear. Given Papa's disdain for a former boyfriend of mine, I was a little apprehensive about whether he'd like this man I was going to marry, but Papa took to Tom quickly, and pronounced him to be perfect for me.

"I could never imagine you with anyone else," he said to me. "From now on, when I think of you, I will always think of you with Tom."

# 50

# After the Wedding

Late August, on our way back to Massachusetts from our honeymoon in Quebec, Tom and I made a slight detour to Brunswick, Maine so that he could show me his beloved Bowdoin College. From a phone booth in the Bowdoin student union building, I called my parents to give them an estimate of when we'd arrive at their home, where we'd stay overnight before returning to Pennsylvania.

My mother answered the phone. "Hurry back," she said to me. "Papa has died, and we're having his funeral tomorrow. Eva's here. She's been here for a few days."

"When did he die? What happened?" I asked.

"I called Papa and Eva that night after you got married," Mum said, "and I told them all about it. Papa told me he thought that Tom is the perfect man for you. Papa was so happy about your wedding! Late that night, he began to have trouble breathing, and Eva brought him to the Emergency Room. It's happened before, a few times, and each time, they helped him to breathe better, and then sent him back home. But this time was different. He died at the hospital in the early hours of the morning of the 24th. I didn't think it was right to tell you while you were on your honeymoon. But we waited his funeral for you."

The next morning, I sat between my husband and Eva at the church while a priest celebrated a funeral Mass for my religion-hating, ex-communicated Pagan grandfather.

"Your Poppa and I don't believe in anything like this," Eva said.

"I know," I answered, thinking of Papa the pagan dropping us off at church when I was a child, promising to drive us home after he'd picked up his racing papers.

"This is just foolishness to us!" she said, her voice full of distress.

"I know."

"What is the sense of it?" she demanded. "Your Poppa hated things like this!"

"He did," I said. "But if he thought it would help to comfort his daughter, he would have put up with it."

Eva paused, her eyes darting back and forth. "If it would help Evie, he would have sat through it, so I will too," she said. "But he didn't believe in one word of it. We've never cared at all about religion. It's always been hocus-pocus to us!"

# 51

## Wishes

Papa used to say to me, may you get what you wish for, and may what you wish for be what you need.

I always wished to be like Papa.

Not in all ways. I didn't want to get divorced, smoke cigarettes, drive too fast, steal spoons from restaurants or bet on horses. And I didn't want to talk so loud nor argue so much as Papa, who was able to win any argument, no matter whether he was right or wrong.

Carrying around a wallet thick with money, as Papa did when he came to visit, or always having a big new car -- well, those things were nice, but they weren't the kind of things that would make us alike.

Papa loved to read, and I do too, so that's one thing. When I was a kid, I thought maybe I'd get four college degrees too, just like Papa did, but I ended up getting three. I loved literature, and I thought maybe I'd turn out to be an English professor as he'd been, early in his career, but instead I taught psychology, as he had.  Mum always told us Papa was brilliant. I don't think that I'm brilliant, but I did okay.

I knew, though, I always knew, that somehow it would turn out that Papa and I were alike. But I admit, it was a surprise to find some of the things I have in common with him.

I remember when I was a kid, we were at the beach one day with Papa and Eva, and I was struck by Papa's bare back. Imagine having all those big moles on your back! It never occurred to me -- not even once -- that he might not have been born with them, and maybe they developed later in his life. But some years ago, when I checked with my doctor about some moles I was getting on my back, she said, "Nothing to worry about. It's an inherited condition. You can probably think of someone in your family who had them."

Oh, yes. Indeed I could.

And the character in his face -- well, I didn't get the big nose, the dark complexion, or the black hair of his younger years. And not his salt-and-pepper bushy eyebrows either. In fact, as I hit my fifties, I was pleased to notice that I scarcely needed to pluck my eyebrows at all anymore. Wow! What a great aging change!

But then, a couple years later, to my immense surprise, suddenly there they were – my grandfather's eyebrows, growing above my eyes!

As Eva often said, "Darn!"

I pluck my eyebrows. I trim them. I try to tame them – or at least to make them appear tame, but it only works for a little while. They bounce right back, growing at a prodigious rate, curling and winding every which way, prompting me to pluck, trim, and try to tame them again. But I flirt with the idea of letting my eyebrows do as they like.

Deep down, and right on the surface too, my eyebrows are like Papa's – wild, unruly, incorrigible, and full of character – that enigmatic kind of character I always wished to share with my grandfather.

# 52

# Evening

They are both gone now, but when I think of Papa and Eva, I picture their ground floor garden apartment in Laurel, Maryland, where I visited them so many times, and we are in the kitchen. Maybe Papa has come in by way of the patio, with his racing paper tucked under his arm. It could be, though, that he comes from his den, taking off his glasses and rubbing the bridge of his nose as he takes his seat at the table. Perhaps Eva is bustling around the stove, licking her finger after dipping it into a sauce, or gingerly removing the lid from her frantic pressure cooker; she may be scrubbing a pot, her glasses riding down her nose; but, most likely, she has just refilled our coffee cups, and is sitting down to the table with Papa and me, dropping a tiny tablet of saccharine into her delicate, and glued-back-together, beleek china cup. Papa has tucked his feet over the rungs of his chair, and is leaning forward, his hands cupping the coffee mug that I gave to him. It is dark outside the bay window, and Eva has closed the small shutters that give privacy on the lower half. The plant light still glows over the long tray of African violets beside the window, and the unstained cherry corner hutch, from which I so often fetch things, catches the light from the lamp that hangs over the table. Cushioned by the beautiful needlepoint Beatrix Potter chair pads that Eva made, we sit comfortably on the cane seats of our ladder back chairs, as we settle in for a long night of sweets, caffeine and conversation. Eva sighs. Papa's voice rumbles.

In some part of my mind and heart, they are always there, and I with them.